Secrets

by

Karmalina

Bloomington, IN  Milton Keynes, UK

AuthorHouse™
1663 Liberty Drive, Suite 200
Bloomington, IN 47403
www.authorhouse.com
Phone: 1-800-839-8640

AuthorHouse™ UK Ltd.
500 Avebury Boulevard
Central Milton Keynes, MK9 2BE
www.authorhouse.co.uk
Phone: 08001974150

First published by AuthorHouse 8/2/2006

ISBN: 1-4259-3830-2 (sc)

Printed in the United States of America
Bloomington, Indiana

This book is printed on acid-free paper.

This book is dedicated to my wonderful husband and to my beautiful children. Also, to all the people out there who have been abused mentally, physically, and sexually. I hope to help the people who have had an abusive life, weathered the storm or not. Hopefully, this book will help someone to realize that it is ok. It is not your fault. You are strong you can survive. You can love yourself; you can forgive yourself and others. I hope this book will help someone to let go of those secrets and to love life and love you!

Yell I survived! I am a survivor!

Table of Contents

Daddy's Little Girl

My earliest childhood memory is being 4 years old and sitting in a circle with my dad. I was sitting between his legs facing men and looking at my arm and letting some man put a large rubberband around my arm cut on one location around my arm. My dad saying, Honey it's okay there will be a little bite, and you'll feel just great, trust daddy, I love you, I would never hurt you, you know your daddy's little girl. I can remember everything being slow and it looked funny like double vision. I could here laughing and see men with big laughs and smiles on their faces. I remember waking up and being hurt on my bottom. So my dad would tell me that I had been messing with my private areas and if I told my mom it would hurt. I would be in so much trouble. Because I knew the way my mom felt about touching my own private areas. As the next couple of years continued my dad had taught me

how to rub myself and try to make it feel good. But I don't remember it ever feeling good. I just felt like it was wrong to do. So my dad took me to my older sisters bathroom and told me he had a friend who's daughter would rub her private areas on the toilet. He showed me how to hang on to the sides toward the back of the toilet and hold my private areas and rub them on the front of the bulging part of the toilet. I would ask if I could stop and he would say NO! You need to do this until your privates feel real good. This went on until I couldn't hold myself up anymore. The pain in my arms and my stomach was so bad. My dad told me to keep doing this as often as I could and my arms wouldn't hurt anymore after awhile. I was daddy's little girl and I did what I was told to so he would keep loving me. Because even though I felt I was doing wrong I loved him more than my feelings of wrong doing. One of my biggest fears was getting caught rubbing myself on the toilet. Because my mom has always said "you never touch your private parts and if you do God will not love you because it is nasty to do that. God doesn't love nasty little girls. So I learned (sort of) how to sneak around. I don't ever remember getting any satisfaction from the toilet. But I did tell my daddy that it felt really good. I felt so bad for lying to my dad. After all he was the only one who loved me. He made that real clear.

One day, I had to still practice, practice, practice on the toilet and my mom caught me. Oh my god the scared feeling I had of her and at that time God. I figured since my mom had caught me God now knew. And God would never love me again. I was now a bad little girl there was no turning back. My mother yelled at me and told me I was the devils child and that no one would ever love me again because I was a nasty, filthy little girl and didn't deserve to have one friend or family member to love me.

My mom was going to make sure that all of my friends and all of our family knew. I came out of the bathroom and went to eat my toast, at the bar, and my mom moved it away. She said no one who is as bad as me deserved to eat the food God had provided for our family. Then she told my older sister Toni that she needed to make sure that all the kids on the bus new how nasty I was. Mom said make sure they ALL know that your sister plays with her private parts. Let them know she is a sinner and the devils child. It didn't matter what she said I was my daddy's little girl and he didn't think those bad things about me. He thought I was his angel. That still didn't make me tell her how I came to know about masturbation. Even though I knew deep in my stomach what I was doing was wrong.

I woke up one night and my mom and dad were yelling really loud. I snuck out of my room to see what was going on. My dad was beating my mom; she was "Please stop Dennis just stop I won't say another word." He told her "Don't you ever say that again."

I went back to my room and I cried. The bad thing is I don't know if I was crying for my mom. Seeing all the blood on her face or if I was crying because my dad was being mean to her. The beating lasted for a while longer. What was bad on my part was I wondered what had started the fight. Was it me? Did my mom say anything about what I had been doing? Did she tell my dad I was a product of the devil? Looking at her beat up face, I felt like it was my fault. My mom didn't say much that morning. The house was silent. I went to my dad's room and told him goodbye I was going to school. I said dad, Mommy looks bad her face is real big and her eye won't open. He asked me "What did your mom say to you?" I said "Nothing …she just looks sad." He said "Your mom didn't say nice things about us and I had to let her know that you are my perfect angel! You just don't worry about nothing your mom is crazy and I won't let her say or do anything to ever hurt us!" I gave him a kiss, and he said he would see me today after school.

Over the next little while the beatings for my mom got worse. Every time they would fight I felt like dirt. I always felt as though it was my fault, even though it wasn't.

I found out my mom was pregnant and she was happy about it. But my dad was angry. He beat my mom so bad I don't know how she didn't lose the baby. My mom called my grandma and grandpa and they came that weekend. My dad wouldn't let my mom take me. So I got to stay there with my dad and he had another party. The "Circle" scared me The thought going through my head was that needle really hurt me, I don't like the way it feels. I told my dad, "I don't want to be bit no more." He said "Don't you love your daddy?" I said "yes!" He said "Ok he wouldn't let anybody hurt me." I woke up in my daddy's bed and I didn't have any panties on and there was blood on my private area.

And when I went to Pee Pee it was red. I didn't know what to do. I just wanted my mother. I wasn't sure why, because I couldn't remember anything. I knew my head hurt so bad. My dad gave me some medicine and told me to go back and lay down for awhile. When I woke up my dad had on an apron and he was cleaning the house. He said "He was going to get my mom and he wanted the house to be cleaned up. I 'm not sure what he said to her, but she came home with him. A few weeks went by and I felt really bad I was really sick and my

mom was going to take me to the doctor. My dad said "No". We will get medicine for her from a friend. Well, he got the medicine. My dad come and set by me and said this medicine will make you feel better.

The medicine was some kind of drug. It made me crazy. I was on the couch for three days and I had imagined this huge white rat about six foot long and about 100 pounds or more, he could talk. He would say tell your mom, sister, and your dad to come here. I'm hungry and I want to have them for lunch. I screamed and I didn't sleep for days. I felt like I had to make sure no one got near me or I would be the reason for them being eaten. My mom would just cry and say "what is wrong there isn't anyone or anything there." I would say Herman will eat you, stay away. Herman talked to me constantly, "Don't you want some water? Or aren't you hungry? Tell your mom your thirsty." He always sat by the couch, or he was under it waiting for someone to come close. After the third day I had lost the Rat. I guess he wasn't getting anything to eat so he went to someone elses house. Even though he was gone I still knew he would be back. I was a terrified little girl, who couldn't talk to God, because I was told I was the devil's child. After a couple of weeks we seemed almost like a normal family. My mom and dad weren't hitting or yelling at each other. My mom was getting a bigger belly from the baby. Until my mom

asked my dad for some money, he got angry and he told her to get some cans and go turn them in, and she could get some milk for us kids. We walked and walked picking up cans. I guess we got enough because my mom and us girls walked to the store and bought a gallon of milk. It was getting dark by the time we got home. My dad said my mom was out with a man named Carl. My mom said Dennis, the girls and I were picking up bottles and cans to cash in so we could have some dinner and the girls could have some milk.

My dad smelt horribly of beer. He was acting so mean he took the gallon of milk and he poured it all over the floor. After my mom and us girls had walked and worked so hard, and there it went on the floor. My mom was beaten badly. My dad was acting crazier than I had ever seen him. He took my mom down into the basement and pulled her down the stairs by her hair all the way down. My sister and I were snuggled up together she was holding me and we were both crying horribly. After a couple of minutes my dad yelled at us to come down there. He said "He wanted us to see what happened when you do bad." My mom was hanging with a rope around her neck and my dad was beating her. My sister was holding me close to her. I wasn't sure what dead was but I thought my mom was, if that makes sense. My dad beat her for a really long time then he told us girls to go upstairs. My dad went to

his bedroom and stripped down naked and he passed smooth out. We knew better than to go to the basement because if dad woke up that would be it for us. We would be bad and that could happen to us. So we just sat and waited either for my mom to return or for my dad to wake up. We were so scared of what might happen next. I guess we went to sleep because we woke up with Carl saying "Come on girls we need to get your mom to the hospital." Carl said "He knew something had happened because my dad called him and said he was going to kill my mom and he would be next. Carl took threats very seriously. So when Carl tried calling and no one answered for several hours he got worried and drove over and found my mom on the floor. So he loaded her into his car and us girls too and we went home with him, it seemed like it took us forever. After several days, my dad came to Carl's house, he was crying telling my mom the drugs and alcohol must have made him crazy.

He said he knew mom wasn't with another man but that just the thought made him crazy. He told her no more drugs so she said ok she would come back to him. On our way home in our van, my dad started calling my mom names. Telling her what a whore she was. He wanted to know just how many times she had "Fucked" Carl in that few days she was there. He started hitting my mom on her already swollen and beaten

face. He was even hitting her in her stomach and he was telling her " I know the bastard in your stomach isn't mine". "It's someone else's. The fight continued for several more miles and my dad was driving with one hand and hitting her with the other hand. My dad leaned over my mom and opened the door, while the van was still moving, as far as he could, he did slow down a lot and then he pushed my mom out of the van. I remember looking back at her and seeing her laying on the side of the road face down. My dad went back and got her.

I thought he was going to run over her, but he didn't he just opened the passenger door and said "get up bitch and get in." He told us girls to just shut up! We were yelling "Dad she can't get up she is hurt!" My dad never got out he just kept yelling at her. My mom finally got up and got in the van. She looked really bad. My dad said nothing to her.

Mom asked him "why don't you just kill me?" My dad said, "Kill you why would I do that?" As soon as we walked through the door my dad told my mom "fix me some dinner I'm hungry!" He turned, looked at me and said "are you hungry angel." I said, "Yes, Daddy!" He said "Hurry up my little girl is hungry too."

My sister was born that April. Right before school vacation for the summer. My mom left the hospital, my dad wasn't real happy about any of it. Amanda was a real cute baby. She had

a head full of hair. My dad said "I think that little bastard is part nigger. But when your wife screws everything in site!" He said "You don't even know who the father is , do you bitch, whore?" Even though we were excited about Amanda being there we were not allowed to talk or show excitement. It was a really sad occasion!

My grandma and grandpa came just like they did with all of us girls. But this time when they left they took my mom and Amanda with them. Toni and I stayed with my dad. My mom and grandparents left. I wanted to go too because my grandparents were the best in the world and I didn't get to see them very often. On my sixth birthday, my dad threw a party and there were probably 75 people there and they were all adults. So my dad had them to bring me gifts. My room was so full of toys that there was no room to sleep.

There were gifts on my bed, the floor, and on the little cubby whole dresser. So I had to start sleeping in my dad's bed every night after that night. Well, not on the nights he passed out or had another women in there having sex with him. He would always tell me to go to the couch. Even though I knew what was going to happen. He was going to slobber on her and put his private parts in her like he always did to me. But I was sad, even though I knew that it was wrong what I was doing.

It was an act of love. I had to show him by letting him do it. How much I loved him and that is how much I loved him.

That is how he showed me how much he loved me. So I guess in an odd six year olds mind. I was justifying what he was doing because he loved me. I didn't think he loved me anymore because of this lady who kept coming over and sleeping in the bed with him.

When there wasn't a woman there with my dad. He would show me he loved me and he would tell me he loved me more than anybody in the whole world. I was beautiful and the only love of his life. He would tell me no one will ever love me like he does. And he promised no one would ever hurt me. Several months (3-4) went by my dad found my mom. He called her at her job and said he wanted to see Amanda. She of course said yes. As long as you bring the other girls so I can see them. All was agreed.

On the way there my dad said we are going to bring Amanda home with us. But don't tell your mom because she will get mad and we wouldn't ever be able to see her ever again. We were both (my sister and I) so excited to see my mom. I can't remember the last time I had seen my mom without a busted up face. I thought she was so beautiful. I just loved her and held onto her just like she did to me. I started to play and touch the little fingers of my baby sister. She was a happy little

baby. I didn't ever know how much I missed her until I saw her again. We were able to talk to my mom by ourselves.

My mom still had on her uniform even her little pouch on the front with a green book in it. My mom said she had to go back to work or she might lose her job. She and my dad talked. I thought maybe he had told her the secret, that we were going to keep Amanda.

My mom said she would be back in about three hours and we would have some dinner together.

I didn't tell her the secret I was real good at holding secrets. So I gave her a long big tight hug and kiss. I knew deep down we wouldn't be there when she got back, or if we were her beautiful face would be beaten and we would still have Amanda. Mom left and she was all smiles even though we begged her not to go. She had too. Dad said "Girls get the baby's clothes and diapers and we will be on our way. I couldn't help but wonder what my mom was going to do when she came home and no one was there. I knew her smile, her beautiful face would be sad. I tried not to think of it. But I just couldn't help, but feel so sad. I cried for my mom. Of course I didn't let my dad know because I was afraid that I would hurt my dad's feelings. I loved him and I sure didn't want to hurt him by him knowing I loved my mom too. My heart was broken…

Then on the same hand I wondered if my baby sister would take my place. Would my dad love her as much as me? Was he going to love her so much that he touched her private parts when she was 4 years old? Or would she be getting bit like I do? As I think back now I found myself feeling totally disgusted about her being the new baby. Was she going be the only love, the angel? Was she going to share Dad's room or was number one still? I was jealous not afraid of him hurting her like he does me 3-4 times a month, but taking my place. It's sad to me as an adult to think I could be so bad to be jealous of a baby. When I knew what was going on with me and my dad just wasn't right and that's why no one could ever know. Dad said mean people would take me. That the judge would be bad to us as a father and a daughter. Because no one would understand that I was an angel. The parties with Dad's friends had slowed down a lot. I didn't get bit very often by the needle. But my dad had a lot of different girls come to our house.

One day I had a friend to spend the night and my dad said she had to sleep over in his room. And she had to sleep in the middle. I was so angry. My dad was going to love her now. Probably the same way he loved me. Dad said "We had to sleep in our T-shirts and panties. Dad gave us some candy (it was a pill). I woke up the next morning and I was still dressed and so was my friend but my dad was naked. I know

this because he got up to go to the bathroom. I don't know if anything happened with my friend or not. It was only brought up one time when I asked him "Dad you don't love my friend do you?" He said "No baby you're the only one I love." "You're my angel my sweet angel" the he rubbed the top of my head. I couldn't help but wonder! But I knew my daddy would never lie to me after all I was his angel. After awhile my dad told us girls that my mom had moved to Houston Texas with another man. Looking back now I didn't really care it had already been a year since I had seen her. My dad said we were moving to Kansas to live with our Uncle and Aunt for a while and he would be back for us soon. I cried and begged not to go. I didn't want to be left behind. My dad told me we were going to be fine to start packing up our stuff because he had received a letter that my mom was going to make us go talk to a judge. And he would be taken away from me. I already knew about judges they were bad, they just wanted to hurt me and not let me daddy's little angel anymore. Dad had our stuff packed and he reminded me of the Judge and "our secret" He said "Remember people will not understand and they will take you away from me." I gave him my word, and promised I would never tell. I would never hurt my daddy and I would never let anyone hurt us.After several weeks my dad came to visit us. He brought along a lady with big boobs. She said "Hello

my name is Debbie and I am your dad's girlfriend, and we are living together, and real soon we are going to be a family." It wasn't a visit from my dad it was an introduction of our soon to be new family. And it was his way of breaking the news that my mom and dad were going to court to fight for us kids to be with him always. I didn't pay a lot of attention to that because I couldn't get that lady out of my head. Knowing my dad hadn't loved me for a while and I felt like she had taken my place. Daddy didn't love me anymore. He loved her!! After all she was coming to court with us and everything. I got so upset I ran out the back door and hid under the porch. My dad came out after me. He dropped my pants and gave me a spanking. He said "I had better be nice to my soon to be mom and except her into our family." I cried and I said "You told me you would never hurt me." "We have a secret daddy, you promised me you would never hurt me!" "So why did you spank me and yell at me?"

I told him " I don't want a new mommy I don't like her!" "I just want us to be a family!"

"Make her go away! I hate her! And I hate you! I'm not really your angel and you don't really love me!" "You have her now. You love her! I hate you daddy!! I hate you!" That night my dad didn't hardly say anything to me. When it was time for bed my uncle said my sister and I would have to sleep in

the living room on the fold out couch. My Dad and Debbie needed the privacy. I felt like a women scorned. I asked my dad "Why can't I sleep with you?" Debbie said " Don't be ridiculous little girls don't sleep with their daddy's!" I told her "she had ruined everything and I hated her too!" My dad yelled at me and said "Be nice or you won't be my angel anymore!" I went to bed and thought how much I hated my dad at that time. I was a kid who had lost the love of her father and it didn't matter that he had me to have sex with him. My stomach and private areas hurt so bad because he loved another person now. And I was no longer the first person in his life. That next morning we got up early and dressed real pretty to go to the courthouse to see my mother. As soon as she saw us come into the court room she hugged us so tight. She was crying and just kept hugging all of us for a long time, touching our hair and our faces and just sobbing. She asked us so many questions "How are you doing in school?" "I am so glad to see you, look how big you've grown, I love you so much!" We didn't answer any of her questions. Amanda cried, looking back that poor little girl was so scared. She was walking and wasn't talking but just a few little words. She didn't know who my mom was. She was tiny when we stole her from my mom. The judge said he needed to talk to us one at a time. My big sister, my mother, and then me. I remember he was so nice not

like what my dad had said. He asked me a lot of questions, but I never told our secret about the men, bites, or the secret.

But what I did do, still being angry at my dad because of him yelling at me and spanking me because of the fit I had thrown, I told the judge I wanted to live with my mom. My mom said it would be just us girls. We were going to live in a nice apartment and drive a car that looked like a mouse. It was a Volkswagen bug and it had ears like a mouse and a tail like a mouse. Needless to say the car was so cute. But it looked a mouse and I was terrified of them. Herman was still a fresh memory! I was always afraid of his return. The judge ruled in my moms defense so it was final we were going to live with my mom. Even though I was selfishly mad at my dad. I still really didn't want to live with my mom. I wanted the woman to go away and I wanted my dad back. I didn't care about the pain. I didn't care about deep down knowing what we were doing was wrong. I only cared about knowing my dad is probably the only person who would ever love me. After all that's all I knew, that's what had been drilled into my head.

A Child's Hell, Now Begins

As we walked out of the courtroom and down the steps it seemed like there were 1,000 steps. My mom was just talking away about all of her plans for us and our life together, just us girls. We got to the parking lot and to our car and to my surprise there was a man there named Rick waiting on us. My mom introduced all of us and said "he was the nice man friend that had helped her to pay the money to the lawyer to get us back." She said "he was a wonderful man and he would be with us, in our lives a lot and she wanted us to like him and vice versa. I remember thinking, "I hope he's not around a lot. And I don't want to him to love me, I wouldn't be his angel!" Because I was an angel to my dad and no one else. Even though I had told the judge that I wanted to live with my mom. I guess I didn't realize that I would be going away. Far Away! My dad didn't say a word to me after court, before

we left. Even though, I was mad at him. I really just wanted to get back at him and the lady, Debbie. Sad to say I already missed him. I didn't tell anyone! I just couldn't!

After several hours of traveling from Kansas City, MO to Texas. We arrived to our destination in the middle of the night or early in the morning (2:00-3:00 am). My mom said "Welcome to our new home!" It was a tiny one bedroom with one bed big enough for all of us girls. Mom and Rick slept out on the couch. I woke up that morning and I asked Rick "Are you going home?" He looked at me and said "Little girl I am home, I live here, and you are living in my home!" We had a family meeting at the kitchen table Rick said "Okay here are the rules you will follow-No if's, and's , or buts." My mom was standing behind him with one hand on his shoulder and the other arm had been holding Amanda on her hip. He said "Yes sir, No sir, yes ma'am, no ma'am will always be used along with please and thank you! You don't speak unless you are spoken too." I could tell this was going to be horrible. My dad always let us talk and be loud if we wanted. That's when I found out there was an inside voice and an outside voice. I already had it figured out it wasn't going to be just us girls! This man Rick was a part of our lives and there wasn't anything I could do about it. On my 8th birthday I had told my mom about my 6th birthday party and about all the gifts I got. Rick

said "You know it sounds like to me you are just a spoiled brat and your use to getting whatever you want. But know this you won't get that around here." So instead of getting a birthday gift he said "you got enough stuff on your 6th birthday to last for several years." He wouldn't allow me to have the box that was wrapped for me. I started to cry and Rick said "Not only are you a spoiled brat, but you act like a two year old." He said "I needed to grow up!" If he only knew I had been a woman for along time 4 years already. So I learned real quick that I am to keep my mouth shut and my eyes in my head. Do Not Speak unless spoken to, never give any information, and never tattle tale. Those were the rules, well a few out of a hundred. I went to the bathroom on evening and I didn't shut the door behind me. When I came out there was a belt across my behind. He was telling me that the rule is to shut the door. I told him that I was to scared to shut the door. Because it was the rule that we were children and we don't work we don't pay bills and we don't use electric with out asking first. I didn't ask! It was late and I had forgotten about electric, Dark time and bathrooms. So he said," your not only a two year old spoiled brat, but your also chicken shit of the dark. Well, after he spanked my ass again. He told me "you don't cry it is not allowed!" He put me in the dark bathroom and told me to sit up against the wall and the bathtub corner and I had better

not move. He said "Not one word better come from my mouth." He shut the door and he left me in the dark closed in the bathroom. I had my ass already beaten and while I was in the dark alone, I wondered where my mom is? Will she come get me out? I had fallen asleep and I was awaked to a man's voice saying "So you moved from your sitting position!" "You will stay in here another night or so until you get it right." So that night at bedtime I went and sat on the bathroom floor, all night! I stayed awake all night. He came in there to use the toilet. He told me to "get in the shower and shut the shower curtain" and I did! He was naked! I peeked around the shower curtain after I heard a noise thinking he was gone. He was looking at me as soon as I got the shower curtain opened. Just enough to peek through! He started calling me a little whore! I didn't know what that was because I was only eight. I knew my dad had called my mom that a few times. So that really confused me because my dad said that to my mom about the baby (Amanda). I knew I didn't have a baby so why was I a whore? He told my mom that I had looked out of the shower curtain on purpose just so I could look at his penis. I didn't know he was naked until I was trying to see if he was gone so I could get out of the tub. That told me one thing. When my mom came in there she was naked too. So I turned my head and I asked her "Am I a whore like you?" She was so angry!!

21

She said "You are definitely your father's child." I tried to tell her that that was what Rick had just called me. I asked her if it was bad. She said "you need to learn to follow the rules around here." "You have a new daddy, you will call him daddy, and we are getting married tomorrow!" We had our blood work done and it is all set! I said, "I am not going to call him daddy!" I said "Mom he puts me in the dark bathroom, he hates me, and I won't call him daddy! I have a daddy and it is not him!" Rick heard me, and he said "fine, if you decide not to call me daddy that's alright. But I do want you to know I won't admit to having a daughter like you!" "And you still will not be a part of this family, so don't expect to be treated like one." I just couldn't understand why mom didn't speak up or stand up for me! Needless to say I spent a lot of time in a dark closet and in the bathroom it was always so scary and dark. I got a lot of spankings, slaps, and yelled at a lot. I was reminded often of how I was not a part of this family. Always wondering what would happen next. My two sisters called him daddy, but I had one, they were treated good, I was not! They were a family and I had no one! Mom broke the news that we were going to be moving to a place called Weatherford. Mom and Rick were going to start their own company. We moved into a trailer park and we now had a baby blue volkswagon bug. I just loved that car, it was so cute with it's white leather seats in

it. I was now in the third grade and I went to a local elementary. I loved school because I wasn't home being talked to like a dog, or being treated like one either. My grandma and grandpa live in Weatherford. I was thinking things would be wonderful if I could make straight A's and I could go spend the night with them. That was my favorite past time. I would sit and look forward to those weekend's with them. My grades were good and I had hope of one day living with my grandma and grandpa. They lived in the country with cows, and a lawn mower. I loved to mow the yard. We would watermelon seed spitting contests and my grandma could shoot a snake right between the eyes. I had the most wonderful grandparents in the world. I loved them with all my heart and they loved me back. I don't remember laughing much at all in my childhood days. But my best memories were with my grandparents. My grandpa was so mild, grandma on the other hand could hold a grudge forever or until you kissed her butt. It didn't matter I love that woman to this day. Always will! Remember what I said about "she could shoot a snake between the eyes?" I was bigger than a snake so think what she could do to me. I hope you realize that was a joke. I remember grandma making Toni and I dresses that were just alike and they were beautiful also a little painful. Sometimes she would get carried away with the pins in her fingers. I would say "Uh grandma that's skin

and she would say well for God's sake be still." I would always giggle and then of course be still! We would get up on Sunday mornings and grandpa would be poaching eggs. No one could make them anywhere near to grandpas. When I was in 2nd grade of course my step dad and I still couldn't see eye to eye. I wouldn't call him dad for nothing. Ever! I bought a monkey with it's thumb in it's mouth and a small banana in the other hand. It was supposed to be for my little sister for her birthday. But I had just bought my best friend! I kept goober. Rick liked Goober too. He would call me names and rip goober just enough to when I would go to grandma's house she would have to sew him up. She would always "child you are so hard on your stuffed animals! Why child why? "I would say I don't know grandma. I didn't dare tell the truth. My heart would break every time he would hurt my goober monkey. I was in the 3rd grade. My teacher had sent home a note with me that said she didn't believe it was me who cheated on the spelling test. I had made a 99 on the test because I had added an extra letter the teacher marked the e out and counted off only one point. "The girl who sat at our little 4 desk tables put together had been moved around the room several times. Anyways even thought the teacher had written what I just did, I was still in more trouble that I could ever imagine. Rick read the letter after of course my mom had seen it. I still to this day can't

figure out why she done that. Anyways Rick said "Ok, now not only are you trash, a disgrace, and an embarrassment, you're a cheating liar on top of all that." He said "Does it make you feel big to cheat?" I tried to tell him that I didn't cheat. The teacher didn't even believe it was me. But she had to send the letter home to both kids parents. If she would have known, Mrs. E would have never sent one with me. Rick opened my spelling book to the first page. He said "How do you spell___ ___? I told him , next word. How do you spell_____? Then I would spell it. I was scared I wasn't for sure if I was spelling them right or not. After the 3rd or 4th page I missed a word. Rick made me pull my pants down, lay over the ottoman that we had. And he whooped me really hard 3 times for every word I missed. By the time I had gotten half way threw the spelling book. I was numb, I had no feeling my arm was in pain, but that's all. Later to find out it was broken. There was so much blood. You know crying wasn't allowed. I had already learned my lesson about putting my hands behind me, he kept on belting. My back was cut open in so many places my butt cheeks were also split. Black, blue, every color under the sun. Rick was tired half way through the book so he went to bed, took the book marked the page and said we will finish this in the morning. You stay where you're at just in case I get a burst of energy. I raised my head up looked at my mom and

she said "Why did you have to cheat?" You're a sinner, you're the devils child. So take your punishment. You're deserving of it. I believed I was the devils child. But I wasn't so sure that masturbation was the only reason I was that evil bad person. Maybe I did something else I had forgotten and no else could remember either or maybe I was chosen to be the devils child. I had a lot of time to think about all that. While I was lying on my chest across the ottoman still with my pants down. You know one thing I remember is worrying about goober. Was he sad because he had to sleep alone? The little stuffed monkey was very important to me. Rick woke up had his coffee and some breakfast. Then walked over to me still lying over the ottoman and asked me my first word. I am so surprised that I could spell anything. I did pretty well. And then, I just couldn't do anymore! My mind was tired and my body hurt so badly. I couldn't hardly stand it. He had been hitting over and over on the places split open from the night before. My mom popped through the living room and said "I'm going to pick up the girls and I'm going to take them to get ice cream. Do you want anything?" She wasn't talking to me she was talking to Rick. I soon found out. I said "Yes I'd love to have a chocolate ice cream cone." She came over to me and said "only good kids get ice cream." You know I couldn't figure out how I got so bad. But I was! It was so nice and warm outside

on the following Monday. My mom and Rick said I had to wear a long sleeve sweater and corduroy beige jeans. They said if anybody was to ask if I'm burning up. To tell them I had picked out my own clothes and you don't have anything else to change into. I said OK! Just putting the clothes on about killed me. They hurt so bad. The sweater hurt my back so terribly bad. The pain was worse than I had ever felt. My arm hurt to raise it, put it down, or to do anything with it really. I went off to school and I wrote with my broke arm and had to keep a straight face. I couldn't draw attention, like jeans and a sweater didn't do it on it's own, to myself. I finally couldn't handle the pain anymore. I asked to be excused to go to the bathroom. The next thing I know I was in there striped down to nothing. Hoping that would take some of the stinging away from my open sores. But it didn't! There was a student that came in there and then ran out. I didn't care. I was still naked and trying to get air or something on my body to feel better. The next thing I know Mrs. E was in the bathroom. She covered her mouth with both of her hands and she dropped to her knees. She said "you poor child! What in God's name has happened to you?" I told her nothing. My parents had had a party and one of the men stayed there to babysit me while several including my parents left. I stuck to that story. You know what Child Protective Services will take your child away

27

in a heartbeat. But they never did me. Remember the devil's child deserves all she gets. The hospital said My arm was broken. WoW! That was a shocker. I was secretly begging inside to go somewhere else to live, maybe with my dad. I will try to like Debbie. I'll try!! Nothing my parents took me home. Not a word was said all the way there. That was ok because I wasn't in to much of a mood to talk or hear anything. We moved to a different trailer park. We had a pink and white trailer ad we lived in lot #5. We had a black velvet couch. Rick thought that would be so perfect for my mom. My mom did a lot of changing. I remember her always setting in her blue zipper down the front robe. Rick would always unzip it and my mom would lay back on him and he would play with her breast. I hated to see that. You can only imagine how the conversations in my house to my mother were very slim to none.

Especially, when you had to look at the person's face when you spoke. And a lot of times we didn't have permission to open our mouth's. I say our mouths I mean mine. I still refused to call him daddy. I wasn't about to let my guard down now and call him a wonderful name like daddy. Rick made it so easy to forget the out feeling I had when I was with my dad, about things being wrong. And knowing people just didn't show love and affection to no one but good people the Jesus

people. When I would turn to ask if I could speak to my mom Rick would say, "You don't want to talk to her you just want to see me fondling her breasts." No I need to ask a question. I was usually told no but on occasion he would say yes and instead of looking at her face my eyes kept going towards the movement of his hands playing with her nipples. He would say "Do you like what you see whore?" "Do you wish this was you?" "Well your out of luck because your nothing but trash. Most of the time I would say "Yes sir and turn around to watch TV. I met a girl that was in the 9th grade. Her mom had to wear a bag on her hip. This girl had blonde thick short hair. Rick said "she was trouble." He had seen me talking to her one day when we got off the bus. She did gymnastics and she told me that she could teach me if I would come 3 trailers down to her house, 1 hour after school. I was so excited I was going to learn gymnastics. I wore her gymnastics suit which was almost like a 1 piece swimsuit. I wanted one to, but didn't dare say so. After several weeks of going and doing gymnastics I wanted to show my mom how I could do the splits. WOW! She said Rick said "you had been down at that girls house haven't you!" The girl wears skimpy clothes to advertise. She's a whore you stay away from her. I was put in my room in the dark, and every hour on the hour would to come and tell Rick "I am sorry, I was bad, I 'm sorry, I'm a whore, and I'm

sorry I have disgraced this family again. It was 6 times before they decided to go to bed. I can remember hearing my mom making horrible (or at least I thought) noises. I sat outside her door and cried for her, I didn't see any marks on her face the next morning. That really confused me but I didn't care to ask either. Since my friend was no longer my teacher in gymnastics I was lost. Rick and mom would get home usually about 6:00 or 6:30. Mom would have time to get dinner and do up a load of laundry since they started there own "Spray on insulation company they would be able to get home earlier than usual. On the weekends we would all go to the Jobs, Toni and I would do the insulation. We wore masks, and would drop the insulation in the hopper and it would mix with glue and then Rick and mom would spray it on the walls and ceilings. Our eyes and eyelashes would always be dusty white right along with our hair. It was a lot of long hours on those weekends they had jobs to finish. I would always be looking for the bridge and the water cause that always meant we were half way home. As long as it was silent in the truck I knew I wasn't being yelled at, told how bad I was or getting hit. The ride home was always the best time. I guess Rick and mom taught me how to work hard and do the best I can at all the jobs I do. Rick and mom taught me how to be different, better, and good to people. That wasn't what they planned, that's

just what happened in my adult years. Mom and Rick would always watch Jimmy Swaggert, a minister on TV. I loved to watch TV, Jimmy Swaggert actually made me cry because he would talk about the devil, satan and so forth. How if you ask God will welcome you in his heart and your life will be better, peaceful and full of joy, love, etc… We traveled to Louisiana to see Jimmy Swaggert. I can't begin to tell you how my heart pounded with excitement it seemed like the whole way there. I was excited like that everytime. I found a deep connection with this man, what he said and how he made me feel. Even though I hadn't been hugged or told I love you by my mom. I found hope that Jimmy Swaggert could take the devil out of me and let my mom love me and just maybe she would give me hugs like my sisters got. My mom gave $100 for a maroon bible that had a snap on it. I was the one who got to stand in the very long line and I got to shake Jimmy's hand. It was electric. I felt peace for the first time ever. I was happy in my heart. Not just excited but truly happy. On our way home I just kept thinking there is a God. And just maybe he will love me one day. I will be really good and maybe just maybe I could be a good person like Jesus and Mr. Swaggert. I remember feeling like I was being held even though no one was there. It's hard to explain but I hope that everyone knows the feeling I am talking about. Rick noticed how happy I was. I

explained to him that I think that one day God would love me and how happy I was. So happy and how I felt warm inside. Rick gave me a funny look and said "Don't fool yourself girl! Your heart is stone, your mind is dumb, your ugly inside and out and there is no hope for you." "God only takes care of his children and You ARE NOT A CHILD OF GOD! At that moment I lost all the good feeling I had. I went to bed and I cried. I had faced the fact that there was no hope of me being a child of God, going to heaven or being at peace. I just really didn't care anything anymore about life. If It wasn't for my grandma and grandpa I think I would have died. I started to really wonder if maybe I did hurt people I was around., if me being around people brought them bad luck. I decided I didn't want to bring bad things to my grandma and grandpa so I stayed home for several weekends. I couldn't hurt them if I wasn't around them.

I Killed My Grandpa

One Friday after I go home from school, my grandpa called and he wanted me to come out for the weekend. My cousins were going to be over at their grandma's (my grandma's sister) They all lived on the same property in the country. So I said ok! Grandpa said he would call back around 6:00 and ask if it would be ok. My older sister went out too. We rode the golf cart and we played hide and seek that Saturday afternoon. We played cards and Oh man it was fun! Grandma said she was going to Bingo and would be home later. That was ok because we were busy being busy! Most of the time I would go with my grandma to bingo. We played hard cards that had little doors you would pull over when you had the numbers. It was so neat. Being twelve years old and being a bingo junkie. I loved the time with my grandma. She was wonderful and everyone liked her. She always wore dark fingernail polish and lipstick

and gobs of Charlie perfume. I thought she was the greatest. I would be so proud when I would sit back in the chairs and watch her carry around that "Old Milwauke Best" in a can with a paper towel around it. It always had lipstick prints on it. To me it was cool. She talked to everyone and when we were sitting at the table would come talk to her. They would always ask about my grandpa. I would always ask grandma during the break if I could call him to see what he was doing and see how he was. She would say yes go ahead. I always did know what he was going to say but I didn't care I called anyways. Then I would go back to watching my grandma talk and laugh. She was goofy sometimes. Always right before break was over she would say "Ok Karm. We need to win big money. I would just smile. See if grandma won she would always give me $5-$20 that was also a secret. Just like the candy she would take out of her purse. I wasn't allowed to eat it at home. But grandma didn't care. She brought it everytime. What's funny is I never really cared if we won because I won every time just being with her. We would always get home late and grandpa would be sitting in his gold chair waiting up for us. Either just finishing his milkshake or finished already and still holding the glass it was in. He would ask did you girls have fun tonight? I said the best. Grandma would tell him if we had won or not. Sometimes Sunday when I would have to go home. I would

hurt (in my cheeks) because of all of the smiling I did over the weekend. What a wonderful childhood memory. Several weekends went by and we had to go to work with mom and Rick their business was doing better. But after those weekends I was able to spend spring break with my grandparents because my cousins were spending it with their grandma too. We played horseshoes, volleyball, badmitten (that golf game). I think that's what it was called. It had colors on the balls like pool balls- but without the numbers. You would hit the balls with a wooden thing and put it threw these rings that stuck in the ground. Boy I was having the time of my life. We had one of our famous watermelon seed fights, my cousin played too. Grandma and grandpa sat out in their chairs, I believe having as much fun as we did. Life couldn't be anymore perfect than that. Well, that last Saturday night of spring break Grandma went to Bingo I went on ahead and stayed with my cousins at grandma's house. Grandpa said "shoot yea the kids can stay down here and play." We started playing a game of Monopoly and grandpa kept us in snacks he even made us all milkshakes. They were the best. He came in the kitchen and said "Okay it's about midnight grandma will be home anytime and you need to wrap it up so no one gets into trouble, including myself" I looked up at him and said "No! We aren't done." I could see the disappointed look on his face that my stupid

ass talked back to him. I respected him and loved him with all my heart. My cousins didn't ride the golf cart down this time. So I walked them home next door. I was kicking rocks in the driveway I said "I'm sorry my grandpa is being so mean." One of my cousins said "I don't want to get into trouble so I'm glad we stopped playing." I told him he was stupid told him by and went back. I was picking up the Monopoly game and my grandpa came to help me. I never said a word to him I was still mad. He said "sweetie you need to get on your pj's and brush your teeth before your grandma gets here. I stood up and stomped off without saying a word. Grandma got home just as I was finished , grandpa was right. I still didn't speak to him. He asked the same thing he always did. He said it had been a long night and told me and grandma he loved us and gave grandma a kiss on her mouth and me a kiss on my forehead. I still never spoke. I was mad you know looking back I know my grandpa knew I was sorry and that's what 12 year olds do. But it still tears at my heart knowing what I did to him, telling him "No" and ignoring him. Not speaking to him. He was a good man. The next morning I got up and my sweet grandpa had me toast, butter, orange juice, and his famous poached eggs waiting for me. He said "Goodmorning sweetheart I made you some breakfast." I said "No thank you I'm not hungry." He sat down on the other side of the little

bar and said "you played hard this last week and you haven't eaten hardly anything. Please eat." I said "No thank you again. Grandpa sipped on his coffee and continued to read his Sunday paper. He looked up and said "will you at least drink your orange juice?" I sighed and drank it. With that sigh I made sure he knew he was asking me to do something Didn't he know I was still mad? Couldn't he tell? And why in God's name was he being so nice? Grandma finally got up and filled grandpa in on all the VFW gossip. Grandpa would just laugh and say "I wish you wouldn't listen to all of that." Grandma was a gossiper. Grandpa never had a bad word to say about anybody. Early that afternoon, my mom(without Rick) came to pick me up. On the way home I said, "Mom I did something really bad!" My mom said "What did you do now?" "Are you going to have it where no one wants you around?" I told her the whole story about the night before, that morning, about breakfast and everything. She let me know what a bad person I was and said now I have ruined it from going out there for a long time. She said "if you are going to treat my daddy that way, I'll make sure you don't see him." I felt horrible about what I had done. We finally got home I had asked my mom to please not tell Rick. She said she wouldn't, but I didn't believe her. She told him everything that night when I went to bed. I thought You know what! I

am going to school and write my grandpa a letter and send him a homemade card. My grandpa said those are always the best, because a person puts a lot of thought and love into a card made for someone he would say its a lot better thank walking into a store picking out a card and reading what someone else wrote. So I was for sure he would forgive me and except my apology. When I got home that day I was shocked to see my mom home. She said she had things to do and didn't go to work that day.

She seemed sad. I felt bad for her. I don't know why I did because she never felt bad for me even through my beatings. So why was I sad for her? Why did I care that something was wrong with her? The house was pretty quiet that night and I heard my mom crying. I didn't ask any questions the next morning about me hearing her crying. But I did ask her if she wouldn't mind sending my card to grandpa. Rick heard me, mom said "yea sure after the way you acted. I doubt he will even read it, much less forgive you!" Rick said "Yea, they don't even like you they just let you come out there as a favor to your mother." I tried hard not to believe that. But I just couldn't shake the feeling that he was telling the truth. I know I'm a bad kid and I'm trash but I really thought until that very second that my grandparents loved me and didn't see me as a bad child. Was it all a lie? Did they really love me? Were

they always pretending to be having fun with me? Did they let me stay because it was a favor to my mom? God I was so hurt and so confused. Rick said "Get going your bus will be here any minute." See I had to wait until the last minute to get on the bus or I had to stand away from the other kids that were waiting on the bus. Because I wasn't deserving of having any friends. I didn't even talk to them when I got on the bus. Kids thought I was weird because I sat and said nothing I just stared out the bus window. When I wasn't by a window I would look at my fingernails and mess with them. Two days later Rick met me at the school bus. He said "Your going across the street with me, we are going to the wayside. I was real confused because Rick was embarrassed to be seen with me, because I was trash and everyone knew. People could tell just by looking at me at least that is what Rick would say. We get there, he gets something to drink, not me of course, because I didn't deserve to have his hard earned money spent on me. I guess he forgot about all the times I helped them on the weekends. I didn't work hard enough to even get a soda, that's what I thought anyways. Rick said "I have to tell you something, Your grandpa is dead!" It as silent!

My thoughts were on the card. I asked Rick if mom sent the card and he said he didn't know. Why do you care? He said I brought you hear so that I could tell you. You had better

be on your best behavior. Because you know how close your mom and grandpa were. I remember his words being distant. I felt so horrible. I couldn't cry. I knew it wasn't allowed even in a situation like this. I promised I would be good. It's real funny because he said you're a little liar, your never good. He said he had given me a warning and that it would be my only one. We went home across the street a few minutes later. My mom came home shortly after she had my sisters with her. A lot of times she would pick them up, not me I guess it was that embarrassing thing again. Anyways Toni and Amanda were crying because of the death of my grandpa. I often wondered if I called him daddy would I be allowed to cry too? My mom was sitting at the kitchen table. I went up to her and said "Mom did you mail my letter and card to grandpa?" She looked up at me and started going through a mess of papers and mail on the table. There it was my letter and card. She said "My dad just died and you are talking about a stupid card?" She held it up in front of me. Ripped it to shreds and said "you little bitch I wish I had never had you!" She continued with "if I wouldn't have had you well my daddy would still be alive." I said "Grandpa is dead because of me?" She said "You were so mean to him that you broke his heart." I said only, but but I am so sorry I didn't mean for him to die, I am so sorry I'm just so sorry!" My mom said "look at you with that smug

look on your face. Your satisfied now aren't you. You killed him to hurt me didn't you?" I said " NO mama No! I 'm so sorry I would never hurt you or grandpa. I am so sorry!" She said "You haven't shed one tear your not sorry, you killed him you bitch!" Your on cloud nine. So not only was I a whore, disgrace, and embarrassment to my family. But I was a killer too. I wish I was dead too.

It Should Have Been Me!

The next morning we went out to my grandmas real early. I have never felt so horrible in all my life. Not only did I have to deal with my grandpa dying, but I had to deal with the fact that I had killed him. How do I face my grandma? How do I face the fact that I was a killer and someone I loved, someone who meant everything to me. Some one who never said a cross word about anybody. Someone who had a lot of friends and was loved by so many people. When we got to grandma's there was a lot of phone calls and a lot of people had stopped in. I couldn't face my grandma. I killed her husband. The only man she ever loved. My grandma had told me so many stories about how they met, how the wonderful things they used to do. I have hurt everyone now. I knew I was trash just an all around bad kid. But I have done something horrible. No one would ever forgive me and everyone knew of me—the grandpa

killer! We stayed at my grandma's house for a couple of days. That was so hard to do Oh my god, the guilt the sorry, the pain was all inside me. Why can't I be good? Why do I hurt people? Why did I have to kill hem? Why? I just couldn't bear to see all the people coming into the church. There were as many people there as there was at my birthday party, several years earlier when I lived with my dad. They were all sobbing even the men. What have I done? These people were telling me how sorry they were. And it was me who should be saying I'm sorry! I never shed a tear. I was the only one. I knew all these people had already found out about me being the one who had put my grandpa in that beautiful casket. I was the one who made him sleep and never wake up. They all know and they are still telling me they are so sorry for my loss. Inside I was yelling. I'm sorry! Please forgive me! They kept saying I'm sorry everyone! Please stop saying that I can't stand it. I 'm so ashamed, and I am sorry. When I went up to view my grandpa, I started saying "Please wake up I take it back I didn't mean to say those things to you. Please grandpa wake up I am so sorry! Please grandpa Please!!! I still never shed a tear! I couldn't hold back the tears writing this but as a child I just wasn't allowed. My mom said "I was heartless!" She said "you never cried! Why?" I said "I can't! She hated me I could feel it in my bones. After the funeral we went back

to my grandma's house, there were a lot of people there. After everyone left grandma's sister said she would stay with her. Grandma asked me to stay. I told her No! I don't want to. Not because I didn't love her. I just couldn't because I couldn't be around her. I was the one who killed him and she wants me to stay with her? Was that some kind of cruel joke? On the way home several hours later the girls rode with Rick and I rode with mom. She didn't say anything in a way I wish she would have beat me, ran me over with the car or something. I was woke up in the middle of the night. There was a phone call! My grandma had tried to kill herself. My mom woke me to tell me. She said "wake up! Your grandma tried to kill herself." "Do you see what you've done? You killed my daddy and almost your grandmother." I said "No I wasn't mean to grandma." She said "You stupid little bitch!" She tried to kill herself because she doesn't want to live without grandpa. She said "My daddy's dead because of you and almost my mother. It should have been you who died not my daddy. You! Do you hear me? You! You should have never been born at least my daddy would still be alive today. I was so beyond pain. I was numb! No soul, no nothing! I was dead too. Not physically but in all other ways. I found myself thinking about my dad a lot. You know he might have given me drugs, molested, and had sex with me what ever but he never cut me down. The

physical abuse (severe) The mental abuse (severe) or the sexual abuse what was worse? Even at 35 years old I don't know I just really don't know. I know my dad wouldn't want me because of how our last meeting was with his girlfriend my soon to be new mom. Would he still be having sex with me? Since he would have her? Do I try to get him by letter? Or the biggest question would he also wish it was me who was dead? Because you know I am a killer! Or worse maybe I had killed him too. I did tell him I hated him and I did tell the judge I wanted to live with my mom, I bet he is dead. I'm so bad, I don't deserve to be alive. I hurt everyone I'm around—I even kill.

Punishment Well Deserved.

Over the next several months I really didn't care about much. I didn't hardly talk and I hated waking up every morning. I always wanted to die. Since I didn't pray God wouldn't answer me anyway. I was a sinner and a murder. Not deserving of love especially from God. We still went to church I always tuned it out. I was a sinner I had no rights to be there. I watched Jimmy Swaggert but it wasn't the same. I felt nothing there was n news cast talking about Jimmy Swaggert's wrong doing with a prostitute. Twice he said he was sorry and then turned around and did it again. I knew he was a sinner just like me. He was no longer deserving of God's love. We never watched him after that everything was pretty much the same. I had my weekly beating got called names, put down, the works. But one day things changed. Rick had come up with a new punishment he decided that spanking me just wasn't enough. I needed much

more because my mom was still grieving over my grandfathers death. You know the one I caused. He told me one day (when my mom had gone to the store with the girls) to put on the dress I had worn when we buried my grandfather. I didn't want to but I did. He put me in the back of his truck and told me to sit, and we went across the street (Main Road) over the hilly part way in the back of the Restaurant and he stuck me in a barrel. It was one on the big tan glue barrels that had a silver clasp on it that went all the way around the lid and locked. Well he locked it and rolled me down the hill over and over. I had no air. I thought I was going to die—even though I was scared to death and screaming. I felt I deserved what I was getting. Rick would open up the lid. It seemed I went down the big hill three times. I felt I was picked up in the barrel and placed in the back of the pick up twice. He opened the lid—I vomited and gasped for air. And he just smiled laughed and said "well you have ruined your dress or should I say souvenirs of your killing day. You know the day you destroyed so many lives. Like your mothers?" I said "Yes sir" I had to go home and scrub my dress to get the glue that I touched (on the inside of the barrel). The barrel was empty it only had some wet glue from the sides. I scrubbed my dress and I got it all out. But I don't know how—I was able to get most of the glue out of my hair. My mom never brushed my hair anyway or even really got close to me. So I wasn't really concerned about

all that! I blew my nose and got all the vomit out of there, and the glue and vomit off my skin. I hung my wet dress up in my closet so no one would know what had just happened. Usually about 3 times a week he would take me to the hill and push me down it. It was a real fun game for him. I wonder where he got the idea sometimes. Was he driving and thought I will put Karmin in a barrel or what? I deserved it so it really was a waited deal, I almost looked forward to it. Because I needed to be punished for my sins. After all I killed him, as far as I was concerned that wasn't enough. I wish he would have just killed me. At least that way I wouldn't have had to feel so horrible at least I wouldn't be around to be a reminder of the horrible thing I had done. And I wouldn't be able to hurt anyone ever again. Rick cut my goober monkey up real bad one day. Right in front of me after one of my beatings. He said " Oh by the way your going to spend the whole summer with your grandma." More punishment but that was something I didn't think I could stand. I still couldn't face her. The first 3 weeks were the hardest because grandma just wasn't the same. She was sad. She talked a lot about grandpa. I couldn't stand it the shame I felt. I'm sorry—I'm so sorry. I said it a million times in my head. But I was still afraid if I told my grandma I was sorry she would be reminded that I was a killer. That I was the who took away the love of her life. I never could figure out why she never asked

me why I did it. That would be the time to tell her how very sorry I was. Words real words not just thoughts of I'm sorry! I stayed out side a lot. Sometimes I would be out smushing cans from grandma's beer. And I would cry. But I would make sure it was a secret. It didn't make him come back. It didn't change a thing. So I'm not sure what the big deal was about crying. Do killers have the right to cry? I was never so glad for the summer to be over. I know I was going back in the barrel but I didn't care. People were still grieving and until they stopped that was what I had to do. In a lot of ways I just knew that it would help people to recover from my horrible mistake I had made. His death and the people I had hurt haunted me 24/7. The hatred for myself grew and grew. The more I couldn't change things the more I hated me. I knew there would never be a punishment good enough for my sins. Only death. I wished to die but it just wouldn't happen. Why? I couldn't understand. My grandpa died of a broken heart. Was my heart so cold? Did I really not feel bad about what I had done? Why? Why couldn't I die of a broken heart? Maybe it's just because I'm a sinner. Do sinners have a heart? If so could their heart be broken? Evil people like me don't have a soul. So does that mean you don't have a heart without a soul?"

Divorce

Rick and mom started fighting a lot. Which made Rick leave the house more often. He would stay gone for hours. But that was ok with me. Except all my mother seem to do is cry. Often I wondered why I was not allowed to cry but the grown ups were. That 's just another mystery in my thoughts. After several months of the fighting —they separated over a women named Lisa. She had stolen Rick's heart. My mom begged and pleaded but no cigar. He was gone! Mother had to get a job as a waitress. Rick came back. It was a couple of months til Christmas so we drove for hours to get there. Rick and mom had gotten a little toy poodle for my sisters. And they didn't want them to see because the puppy was from Santa. So I was the chosen one to ride in the back of the truck. The puppy had several blankets and mom gave me a blanket to put over me. Boy I tell you I froze, but it was ok.

I figured I wouldn't get to play with the puppy that often so I held on tight and loved her. Christmas came and left and so did Rick again. The last time Rick left my goober monkey was ripped up pretty good, so grandma could have fixed it. But I just couldn't call her. Instead I got a bunch of bandaids and fixed him myself. One day goober just disappeared. I would lay in my bed and cry and cry. I know it's stupid to love a stuffed animal but I couldn't help it. I started to find it easier to be able to cry at night. But I didn't let anyone hear or know. (Another secret) I felt better, then guilty because I felt better. We moved into an apartment and there were roaches falling off the ceiling into our cereal bowls. It was so gross. The apartment was always real clean, it was just always full of bugs. Mom worked really hard to pay the bills. She started to take us to church on Sunday's. I liked the people there. I would actually get into the music, singing, and even some yelling(Rejoicing) There were a lot of kids who attended that church. These kids didn't know me, they didn't know I was bad and they didn't know I killed anyone. So I was hopeful of maybe getting to have a friend. Wow a real friend. The more we went to church the more I enjoyed. A lot of my guilt about being a sinner was going to change. I was going to find God and make him listen to me. I hear "do the lord's work." So I decided to cut up some notebook paper into squares, put them

together. Staple around it and fill them with rubber bands. I tell you I went door to door selling them $1.00 a piece. I told the people when they opened their doors that I was working for God. Would they buy so I could give it to the church. I sold all I had. I made about $12.00 I gave to the church offering. I was so proud of me. It was amazing to be so proud of me. I had hated myself for so long. It was like a brand new thing to be proud of me. I helped God and maybe he would get me a couple of spare minutes just to talk. I needed to tell him to tell grandpa I didn't mean to break his heart so he would die. I figure if God could understand he would get grandpa to understand too. Mom worked a lot and so I had more time to try to read the bible and most important understand it. The more I would know about God the more chances I would get to talk to him or at least maybe have him to hear me. As time went on things started to get better I was a teenager now and I was new at school. My past and my present weren't ever brought up. If I told no one would talk to me again. I started to find myself laughing and having a lot of fun with kids at school. I was almost normal. I even started to want to spend more time at my grandma's. She was going to Bingo. Again, and having a really good time. It really made me feel better about the killing (if you can understand). Mom wasn't home much even on nights she was off. I found out later what she

was doing. We moved again more out of town and the house only had a few bugs. It didn't talk long and we had them all gone. My mom had a lot of men in and out of our house, her bed. Then another one so forth. Boy she liked the men. Oh well, she didn't hardly have a thing to do with me, but I was used to that. I started always staying in my room, 13 years old, that was normal. I was making more friends.

Revolving Door

You couldn't ask for a better friend because I could keep secrets better than anyone. My mom met a man at church. She married him! This was her # 4, she was married once before my dad. My grandma told me when I was in my 20's. He was a weirdo—after spending a lot of money on a wedding she leaves him. I wouldn't have looked at him in the first place. So mom went on the prowl for another one. Boy the men who can in and out our revolving door. We moved again only next door. I had my own room. Mom got her hooks into another man. This one was so nice. He treated her like a queen and he had money. He liked me when mom would raise hell with me. He would say "Please treat her with respect." She said "She is a whore and she doesn't deserve respect." He had a real long talk with her. And let her know that wasn't right. And he didn't want to hear anything like that come out of her

mouth again. I told him "thank you!" The very second I had a chance. I told him that I wasn't a very nice person and he told me he thought I was one of the nicest people he had ever met. How could that be? He could see—I just didn't understand. Of course my mom would go and ruin that. She had told me I could go to spend the night at a friend's house and I did, but she told my step dad that I had stayed out all night. Her word against mine…I lost. But in an odd way I think he believed me. Jason and mom split up! Well, my mom came in one day and said your going to live with your dad. I've called him and I have you a ride to the airport. Here are all your clothes you can take and $3.00. I was gone from the house a couple of hours. I had just turned 14years old. My dad wouldn't even know who I was. I don't even know if I would remember his face. I had never been on a plane before so I wasn't sure what to think about it. DFW is a huge place. The planes were huge I had never seen one that close. I felt like an ant. But it was wonderful. Since I was alone, I figured I could pass as a grown up. So when the lady come around I told her give me a Milwaukee light in the can with a white napkin around it. Well, that's what grandma had always done. It didn't work— she gave me a coke instead. I arrived in Little Rock and was so scared and excited. I didn't want to move out of my seat. This would have been a great time to have that beer. I saw my

dad, but I really didn't know how to act or what to say. So I just waved my hand a little. He said "Baby girl I knew that was you!" My dad really didn't look much different—just older. He hadn't been with Debbie for a long time. He had another wife and two sons, ½ brothers of mine. Cool!! He had a house that was on the second floor and the garage and stairs where on the bottom. That was so cool. I thought. Wow here with new people, my step mom, half brothers, and step brother, and sister. A big family, a noisy family, they talked and talked but I never got tired of hearing them. It was beautiful. Dad was gone a lot because he had his own construction company. I suppose he bought it with all his drug money. My dad made and dealt drugs for many years. I was okay who was I to say anything. Soon after being there my dad had already started in on the beatings on my step mom. She didn't deserve that. I felt sorry for her. I liked her and I liked them all.

He said "Angel get your bags together we are leaving." "Go tell he Teri bye. I went into the bedroom and she was laying on the floor her hands over her face and crying. I went over to her bent down and said "I am sorry" I didn't tell. I didn't! She said "I know honey!" I know, go now before your dad comes to get you. I turned looked at her as I was leaving. And said "Remember Saturdays, and remember I will baby sit." I love you! She said "Go just go now "Still crying! I didn't

want to go, but I knew I had to. I walked out and dad was opening another beer from the fridge. He said "Are ya ready?" Yes we left down the stairs to the truck. I kept looking at the bedroom window for as long as I could see. When the house was out of sight I asked dad where we were going. Dad's wife, worked at her parent's store. (Later I found out she remarried and took over both stores her parents owned) Dad hated it, the thought, she flirted. But she didn't! She lived there her whole life and knew everyone. So yea she would say Hello and talk a little too some people. I know because when the other kids would go to the grandparent's house I would go to the store with Teri (dad's wife). She would always give me a free coke, bag of chips, and a ham sandwich with cheese. I put it in the microwave, and heated it up. It was so delicious. I really liked Teri she was always so nice to me and it was real. She didn't be nice to me because I was dad's kid, but because she liked me…for me. Teri would let me baby-sit the bigger kid and the two little ones she took someplace else. I had responsibility. I liked it! Ghostbusters's was a popular song back then and I would get the kids to jump around and dance with me, and we would yell out Ghostbusters. Then laugh when we were done. (Real good memory) Just thinking about that makes me laugh. There was also a song called "Proud to be an American or something like that and we would get up

on the kitchen chairs put our right hand over our hearts. And sing the song. My favorite part, where at least I know I'm free. FREE! I felt free! Not guilt free totally, but free. Free from name calling, dirty looks, being hit, yelled at, and accused of things I had no part of. Everything, it didn't last long. I should have known it wouldn't. Kids like me, good things; well they come for short periods and go away. Teri wanted me to go to the store with her one morning. She said she was going to take the kids to her mom and dads. I said ok! I would love to go—can I have a coke, ham sandwich, and a bag of chips? She said yes you can have two if you want. When we got to the store, Teri let me eat, and said I need to talk to you about a couple of things. She said she was tired of getting hit by my dad and she was going to ask him to leave. She continued to tell me that wasn't my fault that this had been going on for 5 years or more. I told her that's ok. I will help you when I get out of school everyday. I will watch the kids for you. I will clean the house. I will even learn to cook so you won't have to. She said No you won't be staying with me; your dad wouldn't ever let that happen. I cried and I said No please you're my friend! I promise I will help you. Just let me live with you and the other kids. She cried. She grabbed me and she hugged me so tight. I told her, tell dad to hit me not you. Then we will all be together. She said "Honey, I would never

allow a child of mine to be hurt!" A CHILD OF MINE! She loved me; she didn't want to see me dead. I wasn't a whore to her. I was good, good enough for her to call me a child of mine. She said listen to me. I want you to know this IS NOT YOUR FAULT" You have done nothing to cause me to go away. She said "I love you!" Oh My God I can't remember hearing I love you since I was a little girl. I said those big wonderful words. I love you too. And let me tell you. It was wonderful (to hear and to say). Teri said the reason why I was there was because my mom had called and said I was doing drugs, having sex, and I was the reason for her divorce. She said she was expecting the worst. And she had got the best. I told her, I didn't mean to split up mom and my step dad. I really liked him. I didn't want him to go. I really didn't. I never said anything about the drugs, sex thing it didn't seem important to tell her, I wasn't doing that. (I really believe looking back that she already knew it wasn't true) I get a good feeling knowing she really truly thought I was good…me! Good! My step dad did too and he left. So I guess it was only the thing to expect someone else to go away. Teri told me she would talk to my dad about letting me baby sit from time to time and come to the store with her on some Saturday's. That made me happy! She wasn't going to be out of my life and neither were the kids. Relief is what I felt and joy. But at the

same time sadness. I had been there for almost 2 ½ months. I was waiting for Teri to tell my dad to go. The next day I got to stay with the kids. We had several flies in the house, I wouldn't kill them though. I had done enough of that already (grandpa). One of the kids had picked up the fly swatter and killed a fly. (I know this is so stupid) But I started to cry for some reason that broke my heart. I found a match box, emptied out the matches, put the fly in it, and I told the kids come on we have to bury it. It is dead! I seen my grandpa buried so I kind of knew what to do. I made the kids go outside with me, to put it in the ground and cover it up. I then asked the kids to go inside. I just cried and said I'm sorry it's all my fault. You know when I think about that now I wasn't upset about the fly. It all had to with guilt, grandpa, and I think my whole life. I now know I was depressed, terribly depressed because I knew I was to blame for all the bad things that had happened around me. I was guilty of it all. Teri said "I wasn't to blame for her and dad." But that day I just didn't believe it. I wondered why she would lie to me. She said she loved me. Is that really what you do when you love someone, lie? You know I was such a bad kid, but lying was something I just didn't do. When Teri got home Dad wasn't there yet. He was probably at the bar (and probably doing his drugs too). When he got home real late that night. Teri broke the news to him she

wanted him to go. Oh my God he beat her, broke things, he yelled called her names. It was so horrible! Dad came out of the bedroom. He said "don't you worry dear old dad has a place for him and his little angel to go." He was right he did have a place to go. My dad had two friends "Bill and Bob" they were brothers. One was married with two kids and one had a son but no wife. They had a house that a family member had willed to them. That's where my dad stayed when he had a girlfriend to entertain (which that wasn't known until later). His friends were kind of rowdy. But so was my dad. It was time to start school, Dad enrolled me, and I would get up every morning with my dad; get dressed and get on the school bus. After 1 week in school my dad didn't get me up in time for the school bus. I said "Dad is you going to take me to school?" He said "NO" He sat in the chair that was in front of the couch and drank beer and he just stared at me. He said "Angel, There has been a change in plans." I have bought you a plane ticket to go back home. I couldn't believe what I was hearing. I said Dad No please I don't want to go home this is my home. I promise dad, I won't cause no trouble. Have I done something wrong? Dad Please what have I done? I can't go dad. Teri said I could work with her on some Saturday's at the store and she said I could baby sit too. Please dad, please don't make me go back. I promise Dad I will be good. He said go clean up.

We have a plane to get you on in less than 4 hours. I had done it again. Been Bad. I was to blame. I kept telling my dad, I'll change I promise just tell me what to do. I'll do it. Dad Please! When we got to the airport, we parked and my dad said "Karm, it's like this I don't want you here. Your growing into a beautiful woman and I just think it would be best if you wasn't living here with your old man alone. He said "he didn't know how to take a beautiful girl like me. I told him dad, I won't ask you for anything. I promise. I can go to school and take care of things at home after school. I can do it. I know how, dad I know how. I don't remember crying so hard in all my life. He said "there are going to be issues you will have I won't be able to help you with! Boy's I said? My period, I already know all about that you won't' have to have a talk with me. I won't ever bring it up. He said NO. There was a friend of his that had said "How old is she?" He said "she just turned 14! The man said "just the right age then!" My dad said he couldn't bear to know that a man (his friend) had looked at me as a young woman. He couldn't bare knowing that I would be touched by somebody old or my own age. That really confused me and I said "gross dad I won't be doing anything like that with no stupid boys." Dad said "NO." By the time we had reached the ticket counter inside the airport, I was dumbfounded. Did I do something wrong or could he tell I

was going too? I just don't understand. Dad showed me where to go, he walked me there, hugged me said "Goodbye" and told me to keep in touch. He said this is the right thing to do. You'll see when you're grown. You'll know, trust me. It was my time to go! So I walked in, sat down and I hung my head and cried. Never looking around me. I was sure that every person on that plane knew. I was no good and trouble. I was so ashamed! When the plane landed, I was the last person off the plane. I was hoping that no one would be there to pick me up. Then I could go back, sit down and go back to Arkansas. I know now that's no how it worked. My mom was there, it took everything I had for my legs to move forward. I don't know why if it was because I had totally screwed up again or if it was because I didn't want the life I had with my mom to be the same as before. After we got into the car we were pulling away from the parking area. Mom said "Well you've done it again. Ruined your dad's marriage and life too huh? I said "yes maam!" And not another word was said! It was a long drive, a silent ride home. That gave me more time to think about all I did wrong, Teri, and the fly, and my dad not wanting me either. What's to happen next? Mom said go get your bags unpacked, there was only one bag. When I was unpacking my bags I found the $3.00, never used. I put it under my mattress, and went into the living room where my

sisters were. My grandma had just brought them home. I was so glad to see all of them. We had a surprise visitor; it was my old step dad. He had been coming over and seeing my mom for several weeks. Well since right after I left. He was a sight for sore eyes. He talked to me. I told him about Teri, the store, the kids, and I even told him how the while we were on the school bus we listened to loud music! How some of the kids smoked at school, they were allowed to there was a smoking area outside for teachers and students to smoke. It was part of the high school. We went there to pick up school kids who had to ride the school bus because for one reason or another they couldn't drive. I told him about he news I had heard on the radio about a country music star hit head on by another car and they didn't know if she would make it or not. Her name was Barbra Mandrell. I liked her song—Country when country wasn't cool. I liked how she said she put peanuts in her coke. For some reason that always made me giggle. Jason said "why would you want to come back here?" I said I was bad and I was in the way. Jason said I don't believe that. How could he not for God's sake I made him go away! My mom said you need to get ready for bed. I have to put you in school in the morning. I said OK and went. I told Jason goodnight and I would see him tomorrow. My mom said "Good night" in a stern voice! When I started to bed I thought I'd better go

to the bathroom first. After coming out of the bathroom I heard my mom saying "You can't believe a word she says!" Jason she is nothing but a trouble maker, her own dad didn't even want her. My heart fell to my feet. Jason said "now you don't know all the circumstances with that!" My mom said "why can't you see her for what she is?" How is it she could pull the wool over your eyes? She is a liar and a con. Jason said "I do see her for what she is and I can assure you it's not what you think and see in her." Jason wasn't there the next morning when I got up, it was early so I figured he had gone home instead of spending the night. I was hoping he would stay around. Jason came back over after 6:00 that night. I was so glad to see him. I think he was glad to see me too. He said "How was your first day in school?" I said I think 7th grade is going to be harder this year than last. Yes I failed my first year of 7th grade. I also was put back in 3rd. I had wonderful grades in 3rd but my mom decided I needed more learning. So yes I was older than most of the 7th graders, 7th grade was a good year at school for me. Home was horrible, but I loved sports. I wasn't very good at basketball, but I could kick some butt at volleyball and track all you could see was my smoke from the bottom of my shoes. I was running away in my mind. I was so free when I ran. Strange yea I know, but that was how I felt. My mind would lose all my problems, my guilt the whole nine

yards. I loved to run! My mom was a bowler. She was really good too. They were having a tournament in Houston or Austin or something and Jason paid for the whole thing for her. He really loved my mom. Later I found out she didn't go to the bowling tournament she had gone to Nashville with a married man. On Jason's dime! That's my mom, user, liar, cheat! After mom ran Jason off the last time was because she had her lover over one day and was caught by the daughter and wife of him. She went straight to Jason and told him. My mom didn't deserve to have him anyways. I knew this time something wasn't my fault. I met a boy my 8th grade year! I had turned 15 over the summer, oh man was he wonderful! He understood me! He didn't know anything about all my bad that was stuff I only I kept to myself. I had made a good name for myself at school. I had so many friends and people would say hi to me all the time. I got a lot of notes wrote to me. Friends, they didn't know me like my family knew me. I wasn't bad! I was a likeable person, at least to them, to me inside was dark, I was lonely and still hated myself. But I never told a single person. I was a fake, a pretender, a person who made people believe I was happy and good. I had a door to my room that led outside! My boyfriend started sneaking over at night and we would have sex. He was my boyfriend for six months, then. We had started getting threats from unhappy

wives. We had one of our windows broke out once. We had a note on the door that said "Whore! I am watching you. You don't know me but I know you and you better watch your back." I thought the note was for me. But it wasn't! I thought I was the only whore. I didn't know other people were too. If you haven't figured it out. That was for my mom and one of the many, many, men she had going through that revolving door. My friend Tracy had a bit of a problem. She did drugs! I didn't know about that until one night I had gone over to spend the night and she overdosed. Not on purpose! She smoked and taught me how. And that's all I knew she did I should have known. See her mom worked night time. She said "Tracy your brother has a date, so you two girls behave. I have to go to work lock the doors and I will call and check up on you too. The number to my work is on the fridge. If you need me just call. Your brother should be home around 10:30 or so. You know not to have any company Right! Yes Right! She kissed us both on the forehead and left. Tracy grabbed me by the hand and said come on we don't have much time. The boys are coming over. Who I said, she said two great looking guys. One I want to date and the others for you! I said "Oh no, I have a boyfriend and I love him." She said fine let's get ready! The boys came over and Tracy and one boy talked, smoked so did me and the other boy. Then they went off to

her room. The music got a little louder and I just sat and talked to this other guy about sports while knowing what Tracy was doing in there. Having sex, I couldn't say anything because I was too. I saw nothing wrong! I wasn't having sex with that boy, only with my boyfriend. After a couple of hours the boy came out. Tracy didn't though. He said she passed out on the bed. So we are going to leave. I said ok and told the boy I had been talking to thanks for the sports talk and shut and locked the door behind them. I went to wake up Tracy to get all the details. But I couldn't get her awake. She was out cold. I got scared and called her mom at work. I said Tracy is on her bed and I can't get her up! Please come home! She did. We took Tracy to the hospital; they were doing all these scary things to her. They had tubes everywhere. They were pumping her stomach. The doctor said she had overdosed on drugs. I said "NO she didn't do drugs!" After a little while Tracy's mom said "I called your mom and she's on her way to get you." You have to tell me everything. So I wasn't much on lying so I told the truth, every detail. I knew Tracy would hate me after that. But I couldn't lie, I just couldn't! Tracy was in the hospital for a few days. I wasn't able to find out what happened to her after I left because no one every answered her phone at home. One day I answered the phone at home and it was Tracy she was home and doing good too. She said not to call her anymore

because her mom had had a long talk with my mom and well she wasn't allowed to be around me anymore. She said she would sneak when she could and call me. She said we would always be friends, don't forget about me. I promised her I wouldn't and told her I was sorry for telling her mom what had really happened. She said it was okay! Well I never heard from her again. I think about her a lot. I wonder if she is okay is she still doing drugs, did she go bad, did she do something with her life. Did she miss me, was she even alive? I wish I knew Tracy did drugs. You know I don't think she did. I think it was something she did. I think it was something she did that one night to empress that guy. I never got to ask her, so I'll never know. I hope the best for her. My mother and I had a real big blow up. I told her I hated all the men coming in and out of our house. She said if I didn't like it I could leave. So I took my $3.00, a few clothes, tooth brush, tooth paste. Pads and left. I was a visitor at the Front Cemetery. I slept there for several days. One day I decided me 'm so hungry so I watched the house across the street for 2 days and when the lady left that day I went in her window and stole money that was lying on the table. I left this woman a note it said I'm sorry, I'm hungry and I took the $4.00 and change off your table and I'm sorry for using this envelope for a writing pad. Please forgive me, but I have already spent my $3.00, that is

all I took from you! I promise one day to I will pay you back every penny. I watch her house later that evening. I just knew she would call the cops. But she didn't I guess because I never saw one. Then I wondered if maybe the note had fallen or something maybe she didn't read I was sorry. I was determined I was going to pay her every dime. I had stolen from her. If she read the note what did she think? Did she hate me to even though she didn't know who I was? That was a terrible thing I did. I did go back to the house many years later just like I promised. But the house was empty and run down. That was a promise I never kept. I still regret that to this day. I hope that lady has forgiven me. I had a friend who lived about a mile from the cemetery. I was on my period out of wipes and pads and bleeding bad. So I walked to her house knocked on her bedroom window and she let me in. I told her I needed some pads and a shower if I could. Andi said "Yes what's going on why haven't you been at school?" I told her about mine and my mom's fight. Andi woke up her mom and told her. She asked if I could spend the night. She said "Yes but I need to call your mom." That was fine with me. My mom was pissed. She was woke up late at night and for what? Andi's mom said my mom said I wasn't welcome there. To send me to my dad's given her the number and said if he doesn't want her I don't care what you do with her. She said "Don't call back here." I

have washed my hands of her. And as far as I am concerned that troublemaker isn't my daughter, then she hung up! Dixie called my dad and he said yea I will get her a plane ticket. I'll call you back in the morning. He did! In two days I was on my way again. Dixie took me and bought me some new shoes, and some clothes. They had a lot of money! Sometimes she would pick Andi and I up at the show in a limousine. They had a driver too. They owned 2 trucking companies! She was really nice to me. I was so excited I was going back to Arkansas. I would get to see all the good people there. I might even get to work in the store and babysit. Things were going to be "Perfect." Didn't dream of what came next!

Another Nightmare Comes True

My dad met me at the airport he was with Bob. We made a stop at the liquor store; my dad bought me my very own bottle of wine called Strawberry Hill. I don't even know if they sell that anymore. It was good stuff. I was smoking too. I had to get one from my dad. He said yea, my little girl has grown up! I said "Hell Yea so I drank my wine" We laughed and cursed like sailors and sang to the radio. It was cool my dad letting me drink and smoke. He no longer lived at that same house. We were going to live in his shop house. The one he ran his construction company from. I didn't care. I was just glad to be away from the cemetery, my mom, my past there and the men of my moms. Everything! We drank and partied every night for a week. Until one night the partying took a terrible turn. Bill and Bob had a couple of girls over.

Bill wasn't interested in the one girl much. But Bob was these girls were 17 years old and a 14 year old. The 14 year old was interested in Rusty the son of Bill, he was only 13. We all partied that night, Bill wouldn't let Rusty! But he was all into the 14 year old girl who was interested in him. He was a good kid. There were a lot of things about that night that I don't remember, but the ones I do! Tear me up often and have affected my life and the people I love the very most. I remember my dad saying he needed some air so we went out and sat on the swing under the carport. I don't know how we ever made it out there. The next thing I remember is being in the long driveway under the street light, on my knees, and my dad's pants down with his penis in my mouth. He was pulling my head, and then would push it down. It was the first time I had any experience of such a thing. I had never even heard of, or even knew people who did that. But there I was doing something horrible. I was saying (well as well as I could) stop the smell was horrible. Knowing what was in my mouth was disgusting and who the person was, my dad, made me vomit. Yes I did with it in my mouth. I can still feel the pressure in my jaws and in the back of my throat. And I can still feel the pushing and pulling on my head, and I can still smell the smell of his body and taste the vomit in my mouth. The next thing I remember is waking up and he was kissing my neck and he

was inside me. It hurt even though I had had sex before it hurt. At first I didn't even know who it was because I didn't see the face. Everything was sort of in and out. And I felt something my mouth and on my lips. I opened my eyes to see that it was my dad! His tongue was in my mouth and what I felt on my lips was his. Of course I was trying to push him off and get him away. But nothing seemed to work. Then I woke up again! And my dad was asleep at the kitchen table with his head lying on his arm, which was on the table. His pants were undone and his shirt was off. I didn't dare to wake him so I just walked very quietly around the table and to the bedrooms, hallway, and bathroom. And first to the bathroom then to the hallway to sit. I decided that I would wake up Rusty, to maybe answer a few questions for me. I woke him he said he had come and went to bed early because the girl had left early and we were all a bunch of drunks acting like fools, laughing at each other. Well, that didn't make me happy I guess I would have to try to forget that's all. Rusty said, I could sleep in his room because I was a girl in the house with a bunch of men. So I said "Thank you!" He said he would sleep in the hallway all night. I was glad because someone tried to come in he would know. The next morning, when I got up I didn't want to leave the room. I was ashamed, curious, and needed to be sure of what I had done. But didn't know for sure, after all I was a

drunk. I came out of my room (Rusty's) and walked down the hallway. Bill was sitting in the chair on one side of the table and he had a cigarette in one hand and coffee in the other. He was a nice person. On the other side was my dad he had a cup of coffee and a cigarette going too. They were just talking away. My dad sees me before I could go the other direction. He said "There's my angel! Bill gets this kid some coffee. Here's a smoke!" I lit the cigarette and waited on my coffee. I wasn't sure what to say because of the night before may have all been in my mind. So I waited for someone to say "Well, how are you feeling you had a hell of a night, didn't ya!" I looked at him and said I don't remember Dad sorry! He said we played games last night. You spilt the beans about you having a boyfriend in Texas and you had been having sex. You're a very naughty girl. That's okay because your old man still loves you. I wanted to vomit. I asked Bill if he had an extra toothbrush. Bill said "Yea, and girl you need one your dad spent 2hours cleaning up all the vomit off the living room floor. I just said I'm sorry. I guess I drank too much. It won't happen again. I was hoping Dad would have gotten the message from that not Bill. I took a hot shower then laid back in the tub. The only thing I could do is cry because I just knew it wasn't a dream. It had really happened! My bottom was sore, just like when I was little it wasn't hurting it was sore. There was a

difference. I was already tying to think of how to get home. I had a bad feeling about my future and a lot of questions too. After I got out I put on one of Rusty's shirts and a pair of shorts. We were about the same size so it was cool. Dad had left in the time I was in there. He met Teri down town to pick up my two little brothers. I had never been so glad to see them too. They were so beautiful. I loved them both so much. We ended up leaving in the big truck, dump truck; dad had and went to the office house. I was glad to have the boy's there for a couple of days because they were like decoys for me. The night dad took them home, it had been three days since I was drunk, I went in the bathroom and took me a shower. I hoped he wouldn't be home until after I was in bed sound asleep. Well, I was in bed sleeping when I woke up with someone taking down my panties after a few seconds I knew who it was. He was breathing on me and he smelt like alcohol it was so gross. I pretended like I was asleep and prayed it would be over soon. I wanted to put my hands over my ears because he would say Daddy's little princess and the grunting noises he would make. Horrible!!! I just wanted him to go away. That was the first time I realized I hated him. He wasn't wonderful like I always thought even though he was having sex with me as a child. I sill had him high up on that pedestal. No more just kicked it over. In my eyes he was as bad as Jimmy Swaggert.

He was hurting me and he knew he was. He promised he never would hurt his little girl. He just loved me. Well, I'm not a little kid anymore and I know that love doesn't work between a father and a daughter like that. He was doing wrong for the last time, to my body, soul and my heart. The next morning I called my friend in Texas, the one who had brought me to the airport and bought me the clothes. But I couldn't tell her. I tried but it wouldn't come out. I was literally unable to say the words. I said "I'll call you later!" I hung up the phone and realized that even though I felt tough and mean and was going to stop it now. I couldn't tell or maybe wouldn't. I don't know. A day went by and my dad had more people over. But this time several girls, a couple of couples, a family, that was my dad's family. Everybody was having a good ole time. I asked my dad if I could take the TV into the only bedroom there and watch it. He said "come here and see your dear old dad first." I went over to him and he grabbed me around the waist and kissed my temple and said She is beautiful, but a real party pooper. I haven't been able to get her to drink a drop in days. My reply was you drink enough for the both of us, Dad. He said "spunk straight spunk." He put his hand on the top of my head and messed up my hair. I said can I go now? He said "go on party pooper." I told everyone "goodnight" and went to my room with the TV. There was a knock on my door

probably an hour later. A girl came in and said Your not a partier huh? I said no not really! I'm only 15 remember. It is not like I've had a lot of experience at it. I was a drunk for about a week. I didn't think that made me a party animal. She said she would like to get to know me better and gave me her phone number. She was 18-19 years old I can't remember. That next day I called her and said Are you going to run around today? She said Yea, I had planned on it. I asked her if she would take me by the store to see a friend. She said I didn't know you had been here long enough to have friends. I said yea I told her the store name and she took me to it. There was Teri. I was so glad to see her. She said girls are you still smoking. I said yea, how did you know? She said the boys told her. I just laughed. She said she had been hoping I would come by to see her. She said she wanted to call but she didn't know if my dad would be there so she hadn't. That was ok with me. I knew she loved me and I was a child of mine, she told me that day. I still felt so happy to be around her because of that one four word sentence she told me before I left at 14. She said the magic words. Would you like to have a soda, ham and cheese sandwich and some chips? Yes I would love it, I told her. She asked how things were going with you and your dad. My eyes filled with tears I wish she hadn't asked me that because for the last few minutes of being with her.

Telling Only Half the Truth.

What had happened had slipped my mind. She said "Is it bad?" I said no he just throws a lot of parties, he is always doped up and drunk is all. She said you are leaving something out? I said no. I didn't want to tell her no but keeping the secret was more important. Besides I thought she would get beaten if she knew. I would never want her hurt, never. My dad had hurt her enough. We had to go, the girl who took me up there was ready when I was about to walk out the doors. Teri said "Honey, get out of here while you can if things get to bad." Well, I don't want to see you hurt, if she only knew. I went back to the counter and gave her a hug. She said "Honey your shaking!" I let go of her, my eyes were dripping tears. I said "I'm okay!" Love you and goodbye. I went out those doors, got into the car and left. I didn't see her again after that, but once. Those words get out stuck in my head. I figured I would

soon. I just didn't know how, like wanting to die. I didn't know how to do that either! We messed around for about 2 hours, they didn't have to many places to go around there. But at least I did get to see Teri. So that's all that really mattered anyways. I was dropped off at my dad's house. I stood and looked at the house, I guess for longer than I thought. Because I turned around to have the girl take me with her. But she was already gone. My knees were weak and my legs didn't want to move. I really don't know how long I stood there before going in. I opened the house door, my dad was singing and had a towel wrapped around his lower half and he was shaving his face. He said "Hey princess, your old man has a hot date so don't wait up I might not be home til morning. Thank God! I wished he would never come back. I went into the kitchen to get me a glass of water and my dad yells "Why don't you bring your dear old dad a beer." I said Okay. Put my water glass down on the cabinet and got him out a beer. I was taking it to him and when I got to the door way, I looked into the bathroom about 10 steps away and noticed he was naked. He saw me and said come on your dad's thirsty. I felt paralysis again. I felt as though I couldn't speak, move, or nothing. I told myself okay he is going out, and he's clean, he wouldn't do anything over and over. I was telling myself just walk. When I made it to the bathroom dad looked at me, took the beer, and

grabbed my hand at the same time. He took the beer out of my hand with the other hand, because his hand was wrapped around mine. Just him touching my hand with his made me wish I could go invisible or better die. Right there on the spot. He took my hand, put it around his penis and said as he was moving it up and down. He said "A lucky girl is getting this tonight." I could feel the vomit in my throat. I was able to get my hand away. He laughed and said "what don't you love your dear old man?" I didn't speak to him; I just put my head down and walked away. There was a knock at the door, thank god. It was one of dad's friends. He had come over to buy some dope. That's the only time my dad would get into the top of the bedroom closet and take out his box. I know because one party night he left his box out. It had pills, weed, and some white stuff, spoon, tie, and the works. If I would have known then that I could shoot up that stuff or eat it and take all those pills, and would have died. I would have done it in a heartbeat. But I was stupid as far as that suicide stuff went.

Torchered

Dad came home that night. He was angry. I thought he wouldn't be home so I was asleep on the couch. When he came in and woke me up. I said your home. He said yea, she was a little bitch and I didn't get along with her. He was drunk and high I'm sure. I said well I'm going to go take a shower and go to bed. He said No you can take a shower later. I said "later?" He unbuckled his pants and he was standing in front of the couch. He took it out and played with it a second, I closed my eyes; he said open those eyes now. I wouldn't the next thing I knew he was putting it in my mouth, "suck it." I had my eyes closed, put my hand over my mouth, and said "no, no, no! I started to cry. I knew better, he was angry. But I still was yelling No, No, No, I won't! Daddy please! No his had taken my hand off my mouth and forced me to touch it. I closed my eyes tighter! No God No Daddy No, he

it anyways. The torcher was finally over. He pulled his penis out of my rectum, and he pulled his pants up. Sat in the chair across from the couch and said "get up and get me a beer, you wore your daddy out and worked up a hell of a thirst." My whole body hurt, my neck, my head from all the hair pulling, and my rectum was bleeding I didn't know that till I went to the bathroom. I finally got up after him saying "don't just sit there on your knees get up!" I didn't have the strength but I knew I had better. I could smell the vomit on my breath. I could smell him on me too. I was just sick, my head was spinning! I got up, went and got his beer. He opened it and I said is there anything else? My head was down I couldn't look at him. He said yes, he reached up and put one of his hands on my breast, squeezed, and he pulled my nipple. I closed my eyes. I was looking toward the floor, head hung low, my eyes were shut.

The Conversation

Dad took his hand off my breast, and he put it between my legs. I was just thinking not again, but this time I would not have the strength to fight. No voice to yell, just dead numb, no feeling. No thoughts, nothing. I was alive but dead. He popped me on the butt and said "Go get cleaned up!" Yes sir! I went and got clothes, started my shower, and stood there crying inside! No more tears they were dry! I don't know how long I was in there if my water was hot or cold, I don't even know if I washed. I remember coming out of the bathroom, dad was asleep in the chair! I went to my room, got into my bed and laid there looking at the window. I didn't feel anything, I didn't think anything! I just stared! The next day I got up around 11:30 I was woke by the voices in the kitchen. I got up, there were people over talking to my dad. It was Jimmy and Jimmy Jr. My dad's cousins. My dad

said "Good morning Princess!" Don't be rude say hi to your cousins. I just put my head down. Jimmy said "Dennis you know how women are they don't talk until their beautiful with all that make up and stuff." My dad said "she is perfect! Don't you think so Jimmy Jr.? He said Yea! I walked off and went into the bathroom, looked at myself in the mirror. I hated what I saw. I told myself in the mirror I hate you, over and over. Your ugly, and your not a princess, your dirty, and your trash. I must have been in there for a long time because there was a knock on the door. Are you asleep in there? Come on out Jimmy needs the toilet. I opened the door, head down, and went back to my room. Dad didn't like that! When he knocked on the bedroom door he said "get out here and be sociable!" I did! I had nothing to say but I did! Jim Jr. asked me about Texas, I didn't want to talk to him because I didn't want to open my mouth. I didn't want to ever open my mouth again. I wanted to disappear! After about 30 minutes of talking to them they left. My dad was angry at me. He said "why was you flirting with Jimmy Jr.?" I said dad I wasn't! But you told me to. I didn't even want to come out of my room, dad! He said you are a liar! You wanted him didn't you? You want to have sex with him didn't you? I said No daddy I don't! He said don't make me teach you a lesson. Don't go there! I said But daddy I didn't! He said "Look at those clothes your

wearing, shorts and t-shirt; you were showing off for him. You wanted him to look at you! You wanted to fuck him, just tell me. I said "No daddy I hadn't thought that at all." I swear! My body hurt all over, my rectum, and vagina hurt so bad that even my shorts hurt me. When I would sit down it felt like I had been cut with a knife from one point to the other. I still had no energy to fight with him and to be honest I didn't care what would happen to me from that point on. He said, "Don't ever let me find out you have a boyfriend, and I will. I know a lot of people and they're looking out for you. He said Jimmy Jr. better come back to this house to see you again. He says you're perfect so he will be back. First off I was woke up by the noises, he's the one who made me get out of the bathroom, his is the one who made me have a conversation, if that's what you want to call it. And he is the one who asked Jimmy Jr. if he thought I was perfect! So why was he blaming me? He said you know when you throw yourself at somebody their going to take what you're offering, so you need to stop coming on to other men. "Is that understood?" I said Yes daddy, I'm sorry and I'll be good, daddy! I will make you proud and I won't wear shorts anymore.

A Way Out!

Dad was gone a lot over the next several days. I stayed in bed. I didn't answer the door or the phone. I kept the door shut and stayed there. Numb, soulless. My dad came in one night and came into my room and said "are you asleep?" I just laid there. He came over to my bed and said louder "are you asleep?" I said "no I am awake!" He said "Do you want to come and have a beer with me?" NO dad I don't feel very well. What's wrong with you he said? I said I'm starting my period and my stomach is cramping. He said Here let me give you something for that. I told him no I had already taken something. He said well, Okay and left the room. I was never so glad to hear a door close in my life. I don't know how many days had passed when my friend Andi called. I didn't say much to her. She wanted to know how things were, was I having a lot of fun? Did I have a boyfriend? She told me that

a lot of people had asked about me, so she asked her mom if she could make a long distance call. Her mom said Of course and let her. I told her no "No boyfriend", it's not bad here. My dad's getting along good, his business is good and we are closer than anyone could imagine. Dad was fine, I didn't have a boyfriend, and my dad's business was going good. She said she was happy for me. I told her I missed her and my friends and to say hello for me. Her mom was telling her to get off the phone so she said "I'll write you Ok! I'll write you back okay! Yes , goodbye! I wanted to tell her but it was all my fault. My dad wouldn't be doing that if I didn't bring it on first, if I didn't tease him, or make him think I wanted him by the clothes I wore. I thought about my mom a lot over the next couple of days. I was home sick for my mom. My big question was why? She hated me! I wan an embarrassment, a disgrace and I caused problems, I killed her dad. I was a worthless whore. But something inside of me just wanted her to save me. You know like a man on his white horse saving the princess from the witch? I had so many mixed emotions I was confused and unsure of everything. You know I totally lost all track of time. I don't know if it was one day or a week. And the girl that had come over and took me to see Teri came and asked if I wanted to go to town with her. I said Ok. I asked her if she had seen Teri she said Yea she asked about you! I need gas so we will

just get it there. Come on girl lets go! I was so glad to see Teri. But I didn't show or feel really any excitement. I still was in a lot of ways numb. When we got to the store I walked in. Teri grabbed me and said "HI! How are you?" I said "Fine!" She said your dad came in and I asked him would it be ok for you to come work with me this coming Saturday. You know she hated to talk to my dad. He said "Okay" I said why are you talking to my dad? He is mean to you, she said honey your worth it. Besides when you're a grown up you'll understand that when two people who once loved each other, shared life, and had kids that they will communicate with each other for the children. She said you're not my biological child, but in my eyes you're still a child of mine. I guess I wasn't too excited because she said "honey what is wrong?" I said nothing she said ok but I'm here if you want to talk. She said are you a little homesick? Yea I miss my friends. Hey why don't you go get a coke! No I'm not thirsty, get a sandwich, and some chips? But thank you anyway! She said get it and you can eat and drink them later. No that's okay! But thanks! I looked down quick because she was looking at me like she knew. I had enticed my dad and not by words, but by actions, asked my dad to have sex with me. I couldn't look at her. She would hate me too. I was so ashamed! I wanted to die right that second. I didn't want to hurt her, I loved her. People were coming into

the store so I just stayed behind the counter and kept my eyes on the floor. After the people left. Teri said child look at me. I couldn't! I just started crying! She put her fingers under my chin and forced my chin up , my eyes stayed down. She said your crying look at me now! I did, I didn't want to make her mad at me. She said looking at my face then my arms, she turned me around and looked at my back, then my front. She put my shirt down and said is he hurting you? I said No! Still crying, No he isn't hitting me! That was the truth! I had not lied to her. She looked at my face and said "Dear God!" He is hurting you isn't he! I cried even harder! She got out a piece of paper and gave me a phone number she said this is my friend call her. Go pack your things and get out before your dad gets home. You can stay with her! She hates your dad you'll be safe there. Go! I hugged her and left the girl was waiting on me. I asked her if she would take me home. She said you upset what is wrong? I said nothing! I just need to go home! I lit another cigarette and hoped my dad wouldn't be home. We arrived and he wasn't! I ran in got my stuff together only favorites. Got on the phone. No Answer! Oh Dear God! Before I knew it there was a knock on the door! I looked out a woman! She was there to get me! She said "Got your stuff? I said yes, let's hurry!" We jumped in her car and took off! She said your dad's a sorry ass! It should have been him that

got the bullet instead of his brother, after all that's who it was intended for! Later I found out that there was a man out to kill my dad. He had screwed him over. I figured it was a drug deal or it was that my dad had hurt one of his kids, or maybe he was sleeping with his wife. We got to this lady's house and she said let's call your mom! You can stay here for a couple of days! Honey but sooner or later he will find you here. I asked her if I could call my friend instead and she said yes! I called Andi's mom and told her my dad and I were having sex and I wanted to come home. Could she please send money for a ticket or buy me one there?" She said Yes give me a number where you can be reached and I'll get you one ASAP!

On My Way Home

I waited by the phone for what seemed like forever, but it was only a few minutes. She promised me she would call me back! The phone rang and the lady answered it! She said "Yes, Yes, Ok, Thank you!" Well I had a ticket but it wasn't until the next day. I spent the night in her kid's bed on the lower bunk and for the first time in a long time I didn't have to worry about being touched. But I also knew that if by chance my dad found me, he would probably kill me! I had crossed a dangerous line! The next morning when I woke, the lady had said Teri had called her. My dad had been at the store asking Teri if she had seen me. She said yes yesterday! She came in with a girl! Dad said yea, she had told him. The girl told my dad that I was real upset and that I was in a hurry to get home. Did she know why? Teri said yea she said she was getting a little home sick. Why are you asking so many questions? He

said she didn't come home last night I was just wondering! If you see her call me, I'll be at home! Teri said Okay! We hurried and loaded up my things. I laid down in the back seat through town and several miles out of town. Just incase I was seen. She gave me the OK to get up. When we arrived at the airport she took me up to the counter, we got my ticket and watched for the plane and kept an eye out for my dad. Just incase he had found out! I boarded the plane and felt a little relieved and anxious about what was next. I now I would have to tell the truth, I would have to tell about how bad I had been. I didn't want anyone to know any more than I had told already. The plane ride seemed really short this time. I know it was because I was dreading going back to Texas. I still couldn't shake wanting my mom. I just wanted her to hug me and tell me it was ok. I knew that wouldn't happen, I knew she would be mad. She didn't want me. I knew that! And I knew that what had happened to me wouldn't change a thing. It was all my fault! But would she forgive me? My friend met me at the airport. I just gave them the biggest hugs. Andi ask me if I was okay. And Andi's mom said "good to see ya and how was the plane ride? I was so glad they didn't ask me any questions about what had happened. On our way back home in the car I was asked if I was hungry. We were going to stop and get something to eat. I said sure. I could eat a little! Andi's mom

smoked, but told me I couldn't! She said I was to young to have such a bad habit. Andi's mom and dad had to go out of town for a couple of days. There was a lady who was coming to baby sit us. Over the weekend, I spaced out. I got terrified that my dad was going to find me. I thought I was going to have to have sex with him again, or he would kill me, because he would be so angry at me. Poor Andi didn't know what to say! The babysitter said "honey I don't know what all took place when you were living with your dad. But I can assure you one thing. He won't find you! His penis can't reach from Arkansas and if he came here "I'd kill him!" Your safe honey you have no reason to worry about being found. It's Okay! It will be alright just relax! We haven't called my mom yet to let her know I was here. Andi's mom said we would do that when she got back. Unless I wanted to call her so bad, but didn't either. I just couldn't sort out any of my emotions about my mother at the time. I would have to talk to her, and tell her soon. After Andi's mom got back from her trip she asked me if I wanted to call my mom that night or if it could wait till morning? I said let's do it in the morning. That night I don't think I slept at all. The anticipation of seeing my mom the next day was overwhelming. That's if she wanted to see me at all. We made the phone call later that morning. Andi's mom talked to her for several minutes on the phone before she hung

up. I was told your mom had several things to do, but after she gets finished she'll come and get you. She said be looking for her because she's not going to get out of the car. Andi's mom just shook her head. Seemed real digusted about the phone conversation. She had had with my mother. The only thing she really said after that was I see why you don't want to see her. When my mom got there she just honked. I gave hugs and said thank you for getting me home, and for letting me stay here with you. I told Andi I would call her later. I walk out got in the car. Mom said "your back huh? Yes mam! I'll never go back again. My mom said she and the dog had been out all day and she was going to stop and get her a bite to eat. She asked me if I wanted something I said my stomach was upset but yea I thought I could eat. We went through McDonald's and my mom ordered two hamburgers I thought one was for me. She took the bread off and gave the meat patty after breaking it off in little pieces for her and gave it to the dog. I just sat there waited to see if (well I don't know). She pulled away from the window – so I knew one wasn't mine. She just looked at me while she was eating on her burger. She said "what?" You never eat when your stomach is upset. I guess I should have known there would be some excuse to leave me out. We got to my mom's house. The first thing I did was go to the refrigerator. I opened the door looked and got me

out some tea. I started to cry, put the tea back in the frig and went to my room. It looked the same, nothing taken out. I laid down on my bed and sipped my tea. My mom yelled at me to come here. So I did. She said whatever it is you say happened there you need to keep to yourself. Because I don't want your dirty laundry to jeopardize my reputation. I have a good name and I don't want you ruining it. My mom said my dad had called her and told me how you went down there and told him how Jason had molested you. And that's why you ran away from home. I told her that's a lie. I never said anything bad about Jason, he was my friend and I love him, mom! I swear I never said anything like that! She said he's on his way over here. He wants to let you know just how he feels about you now. Jason got there and I was so ashamed even though I had said nothing bad about him ever. I felt like I had done it. Because I was told I did. Jason said, did you say those things your father said you did? I said No sir. I swear I didn't. I was crying so hard. I didn't want him to think badly of me. I didn't do it. He looked at me and he said Okay! I believe you! I told your mother I thought the story your dad said was far fetched and unbelievable. I hugged him so tight and said thank you for believing me, I would never say anything like that about you. After Jason left, my mom asked me "How do you always pull the wool over that man's eyes? I said because

97

I didn't lie to him I've always told Jason the truth. He is my friend! No – he's not your friend. What is it that you really want him to be? Your lover maybe? I told my mom that was gross! And she shouldn't say that. She said I know your type. Honey you can't fool me. So who did those things to you? Your Dad? He told me you were having sex all over town, and you were wearing skimpy clothes. You was also partying all the time, and coming in at all hours of the night. Then of course the lies you were telling. He said he tried to get a handle on you but couldn't! Damn, why do you have to act this way? She told me one screw up and I was gone. She said she wasn't at all thrilled about me being there in the first place. Looking back on things my dad had told my mom that to save his own but, and about Jason—well he said that so they wouldn't believe the story when I told what he had done to me. He did a great job of convincing my mother. But he failed when it came to Jason. He believed what I said! He never heard my side of what happened no one had. All they knew is I had to have sex with my dad. As far as I was concerned that's all anyone had to know. My sisters got home from school. I was so glad to see them and they were glad to see me too. I hoped they would never find out what I'd done. If I could help it, they never would. They knew something was going on because I guess I had changed and it was obvious. Mother said she was

going to enroll me into school on Monday. I said great! I hoped Andi hadn't said anything to anybody. I didn't think she would, but I wondered anyway. Starting school was a good thing for me. My old friends were still my friends. I loved sports; it was a release for me. My mom still had the revolving door. He and my oldest sister had to see all the men. Because I didn't want to go live with my dad again. And I knew that would happen. Mom went to my oldest sisters out of town games and since I had after school practice I couldn't go. My mom asked Jason to come watch us, my little sister and me. I was so glad to see him. I asked him why he believed me. He said your mom had told me about the life she had with your dad. She told me that on their wedding night my dad had hired a hooker- to show my mom how to do things the right way. She had told him all about the lies, beatings, jealousy, and so forth. Oh I see! He said he told my mom she was wrong for letting me go there in the first place. But she said "she made her bed now let her lie in it." You know that saying has never made any since to me. If you made your bed, why on earth would you lie in it? Anyway I went and stayed at my grandma's house that weekend. My grandma said "Karm, why would you say such horrible things about Jason? I told her I didn't. Jason believes me she said you know if you have problems maybe we could talk about them and you wouldn't have to go around

spreading those lies. You know what you said about your dad making you have sex! Isn't true either. Dad's don't do things like that with their little girls. I told her my dad does! She said you really need to get some real help from somebody! These things you're making up have to stop. I said Yea, Maybe your right! That was the first time it hit me! NO ONE BELIEVED ME and if my own grandma didn't! She always loved me. But maybe because I killed grandpa she was still mad. Maybe she just said those things to hurt me. Playing Bingo that day wasn't very fun for me, it lasted forever. When grandma and I got to her house that night she said are you tired? Yea a little bit, when we walked into the house the first thing I had seen was my grandpa's chair. I just wanted him to be sitting there and say "hey how was you girls night? Drinking on a milkshake or just finishing it up, holding the glass in his hand. But those words would never be said again. And it was all because of me. Grandma said do you want a milkshake? I said sure, she made us one and I sat on the couch looking at my grandpa's chair. Just saying I'm sorry in my head. Grandma had been talking to me, but I couldn't tell you one word she said. My thoughts were on my grandpa and all the bad things; I had brought on so many peoples lives. Especially my grandma even I'm sorry couldn't bring him back. We went to bed after a little while, I got back up because I was just looking at the ceiling anyway.

I hadn't sat in grandpa's chair since his death. I sat down in grandpa's chair and I just thought. I kept looking over at the gun standing up by the front door. I went over and picked it up and took a good look at it. I thought if grandma tried to kill herself with it. Then there was a way I could too. I examined it good, put it to my heart and pulled the trigger, but it wouldn't work. Later I found out guns had a safety on them. Damn I was mad. Why didn't it work? How did I screw that up too? That's all I ever did was mess everything up. I decided to go back to bed and look at the ceiling a little more. Got up the next morning and grandma asked me if I wanted her to make some potato soup. I said Yes, I would love that! She asked do you want a couple of poached eggs and toast. I said No thanks I'll just have toast and orange juice. That brought back the memory of the last Sunday morning with my grandpa. How I wouldn't eat the eggs he had made for me. I wish he was there, with me right then. I would never say anything wrong to him again. I would never break his heart. That way he would never die. I knew though I was dreaming. The guilt of my grandpa had been with me for 4 years now. And instead of it going away some it only got stronger. Grandma has gone on with her life, I was glad. She laughed and had a real good time at the VFW that night before. I was the one who was miserable. But that was away

of life, a path I chose. A decision I would live with forever. If I had only done what I was told instead of being mean to him. Everything would be ok.

Running Away – Getting Married

Mom came out to grandmas to get me. I wasn't looking forward to that. On our way home she said Grandmother said she had talked to you about your lies. I have talked to you all your life about that, and you still do it. Did your grandma talk some since into your thick head? I said yes! She said I don't know why god continues to punish me, with you. My mother always told me you'll get back with your children, the way you are with me. That made me wonder was my mom a bad child. Is that why my grandma told her that when she was growing up? My mom said I've paid enough for the hell I put my parents through. I shouldn't have to be paying anymore of my mistakes. My mom must have really been trouble. I wondered if she was as bad as me. I wondered if she ever killed anyone. But I didn't dare ask. My mom said me and your grandma

couldn't see eye to eye on anything when I was growing up. If I came in 20 minutes late. I was off doing something I shouldn't have been if Uncle Earl came in an hour late it was ok. Earl has always been mothers favorite, he was perfect. I was nothing in mother's eyes. Daddy would always believe me when I told him why I was late. I wish she would have listened to what she had just said to me. Your grandma always says Karm is the best kid out of the whole bunch. I don't see why you're always so hard on her; she said I can't even be a good mother—in my mother's eyes. I found myself feeling sorry for my mom. She just wanted to have a good relationship with her mom. I tried to tell her it was okay she was a good mom, and grandma thinks so too. Why on earth would I try so hard to make her feel better? She never had me. After about 2 months of me and my mom at each others throats I decided I couldn't handle it anymore. She was constantly on my butt about everything. She told me that I was just jealous of her men friends. That I was the one who was wrong. I never wanted her to be happy. And she wasn't going to be unhappy for me. So guess what, I packed up my stuff walked to my friend's house and asked if I could move in and did. Her parents were really strict, but that was okay with me. I had someone to talk to at anytime if I did need to. I would never go back to my mom's again. Never!! I had a friend, male; we had been friends for a while. He was

older, he was 18, but that was okay we were only friends. He used to come over and I would sneak out with him, so I could ride on the back of his motorcycle. It was so much fun. He was my best male friend; we had a lot of fun together. My friend ended up getting pregnant. So she got married and I moved in with my friend, Marcus. His parents didn't want any accidents like what happened with my friend. So ended up having to get married. That day I called my mom and said I want to get married, but since I am only 16 I have to have you sign. She met me up at the courthouse, signed and I was married. And out of my mom's hair. I was a married woman. We, Marcus and I went back and forth about having sex because we were good friends. We did and that ruined everything-our friendship was no longer. He was jealous of all boys-men. And he didn't let me get a job. I couldn't drive, I didn't have a license, and I really wanted to work. But men would be looking and talking to me. He wouldn't hear of it. Our relationship went sour real quick. Marcus knew I was sexually abused at 15, but he didn't know the extent of it and he also knew nothing from before that. When we would get into an argument, which was usually over me talking to someone else. He would knock the shit out of me. When we would be home if we wasn't already—he would take me to our room in the basement, and hit on me until he would get so excited he

would want to have sex. He'd say yes, you fucked your own daddy and I'm your husband, and you won't do it with me? He ripped my heart out every time he would say those words. The beatings got worse, his thing was-the phone-the part you talk on. He would beat me in the back with it. That way his parents wouldn't see any bruising. It didn't take much longer and I was gone. I had become my mother. I was abused by my dad-married someone who was like him. I had to go to my mom's on bended knees and ask to stay with her. She let me! My oldest sister was moved out. She left like me because of my mom and her men. And how it just wasn't good for my kid sister to be around all that! They still haven't spoken in 20 years. My sister has 4 kids and my mom hasn't seen any of them, only by pictures that people have shown her. My mom bought her a house; I helped to move into it. And I had my own room, it was a real cute house, there were enough bedrooms with my older sister being gone. I was now 17 and I had a curfew of 10 p.m. That didn't set well with me. I had to follow rules because I had no where else to go. I can still remember the day my divorce papers were delivered. That was so upsetting to me 17 married and now divorced already. I had friends and still went out a lot and yes home by 10p.m. One night when I was out with some friends, we was drinking and having a great tie at the lake. I didn't go home until 10 the next morning.

My excuse was you just said 10:00 you didn't say that night or the next day. Well, I was a horrible child but of course I always had been. The whole time I was hearing about how I was out drinking and whoring around I couldn't help it. I just couldn't keep a straight face. That pissed her off even more. After a month of that bullshit I moved out. I moved in with a lady named Suzy. That's when I met my husband, Allen. The most wonderful thing in all the world and he still is. I told him about how I had had sex with a lot of people, and that I didn't get along with my mom, and that I had been married before. Even though, I was only 18. I told him about how I didn't care if the man was married or not. I hated myself. We had never been out on a real date. Within 3 weeks of meeting him we were married. He said he knew from the second he saw me that we would be together. He Loved me. I didn't tell anyone in my family that I had got married. His family was all at the church when we did—but none of mine. To me it wasn't that important that they knew. After 1 month of being married I went and knocked on my mother's door. Asked if my little sister was home, she said no not yet. She asked me in. I told her I was married again to a really great guy. She said "What a shame your 18 and been married twice. I said yes- what is funny is I didn't even know how to spell his last name when we got married. But mom he loves me and that's all that

matters. Do you love him? I said yes I 'm trying! Well you'll be divorced again by the time your 20. So when do we get to meet him? I said I'll bring him by tomorrow, tell Amanda I came by. I will see ya'll tomorrow. I told my husband that I went by my mom's and I wanted to go by there tomorrow after he got off work. He said Okay! Whatever you want to do! The next day we went over to my mom's so her and my little sister could meet the man who loved me for me…enough to marry me and give me his name. I wasn't going to ruin this like I did the first one by telling secrets I had held onto for so many years. My sister really liked him and so did my mom. She told me try not to screw this one up. Be on your best behavior so he won't know about your trashy life you've lead, another word of advice. Don't mix up your lies keep them all straight, so you don't lose him. I should be telling you not to lie, but I know with you that is asking to much. I told her I don't lie to him so there are no lies to keep straight. This man makes me feel safe, he is my protector and he loves me. My mom said that's all good for now. But once he sees your true colors he'll run. Girls like you just don't get good men. She said tell me something! Who's going to protect him from you?

Men First Always

Well as the night went on my mom said she had met a wonderful man. His name was Dale. She said he would be over soon. He has money, he is good looking, and he's good to me. I said great we can't wait to meet this Mr. Wonderful. He came in shortly. Mr. Wonderful was drunk the smell of beer was strong. I didn't think he was good looking at all. And as far as the money thing—who really cared. He made a poor impression on me but I didn't say. I smiled and was nice to him. He asked my husband if he wanted a beer he said sure a cold one would be nice. We stayed for about 3 hours and then we went on home. I just loved my little sister who was 12 ½ years old, she was precious. I felt bad for her though. Several months past and I was going over to visit on a regular basis. My mom and I got along pretty good. As long as I listened to her cut me down. We got along great. My husband went

over there a lot with me when he got off work. He never had a bad word to say. He was a good man, he reminded me of my grandpa. One day I was over there and my mom was really sick, vomiting, diarrhea, fever, the works. Dale was out at the bars, Amanda was at some camp for the weekend and mom was all alone. I called my husband at work and said my mom was real sick. I was going to stay there all day to take care of her. Would he get a ride there or walk it wasn't but 3 blocks away from his job. He said yes! I sat with my mom, wiped her head and neck with a cool wash rag. Helped her to the bathroom to go potty and cleaned up all the BM off the carpet and her bed covers. I changed her bed 2 times while I was there. I cleaned the floor several times. I'd help her back to bed and try to get warm tea down her. I would set on her floor, by her door way while she slept, just in case she needed anything. Hours went by and Allen had already got there. I had tried several times to get a hold of Dale but no luck. He finally called around 7:30 pm and said he would be over later. I could tell he was drinking. I explained to him mom was really sick, so he might not want to come over. I told him we would stay the night with her so it would be no problem for him to go on home. He said "No I'll be over in an hour. Around 12:30 that night he finally drove up. He told us thanks for staying with her and he would take care of her now.

I said OK I'll be back over about 8:30 in the morning. I was there just like I said I'd be. I went straight upstairs to see how my mom was doing. She seemed to be doing better. I asked if Dale spent the night she said yes. I said did he help you a lot? She said No he was to drunk. I about died! I said what? She said the only reason he was here was because he was horny. I said did he get mad when you told him you were to sick to have sex? I mean my God you could see that just by looking at mom. Damn. I could have stayed if I knew he wasn't going to help you. Mom said after they had sex he went to sleep and she wasn't able to get him up to help her out. I was pissed. I said mom I am so sorry, I didn't know. Mom said the sex wasn't what she wanted, but he did it anyway. The more she talked the madder I got at that SOB. How dare he do that to my mom! I had already decided that as soon as he got there I was going to let him know that he needed to go away and never return. I was never able to stand up for my mom and I still carried around the guilt of not being able to stop her beatings with my dad. Or stop the hanging in the basement or being pushed out of the van going down the highway. I was damn sure doing something about this.

Go Away and Never Let Me See Your Face Again.

Dale got there at around 4:00. Mom was able to keep down some soup I made her and crackers. She was feeling much better, but still very weak. Dale came in and said "How are ya feeling?" Mom said better Karm made me some soup and crackers. I'll get my strength back and be good as new. I couldn't hold my tongue any longer. This guy coming in acting so concerned. I said Look you need to go on and stay gone. I'll take care of my mom, we don't need you here. He said are you going to sit there and let this little bitch talk to me that way? My mom told me to shut up there wasn't any reason to talk to him that way. I said mom your sick you vomited and shit all over your bed and the floor. I had to change your sheets twice and clean up the floor bunches of times on the way to the toilet. What do you mean for me to shut up? Dale said

112

don't think your going to make me go anywhere. Your mom doesn't want you around anyway so you go. I said No you had my mom to have sex with you knowing how sick she was. Your mom wanted it. So you go to hell! I said Mom would please ask him to leave? She looked right at me and said no you need to go if you can't respect the man I love in my own home you need to go and never come back here again. I couldn't believe what I was hearing from her. I said mother, you don't know what you are saying! Your sick and not thinking straight, I'm here to help you! She said you've never helped anyone in your life; you've never wanted me to be happy. You just can't stand that I have a man who loves me and makes me happy. I know what I'm saying I'm not that sick. She said go —and don't ever let me see your face again. You've been trouble since you were born and you still are. I walked out, went to my car, drove around and tried to make heads or tales of what had just happened. What did I do? What just took place? I thought I was doing right by her. Why do I always screw up everything? Why can't I be good? Why must I always hurt people? I had to go pick up my husband at 6:30. He asked about my mom and he asked if I had been crying. What's wrong he asked? I told him the whole story. He said don't worry about it you did the right thing. Your mom will call you later and say she made a mistake and she's sorry. No she won't, I thought! We

got out to his dad's house and by that time I knew how to commit suicide, just take a few pills that will do it. I stole a bottle of Tylenol but there wasn't hardly any in it so I asked Allen if he would go get me some. He said sure! When he got back I told him thanks and went and locked myself in the restroom. My husband went over to my sister's house that lived right behind my mom. The one who hadn't talked to her in a couple of years, at that time. She said she wanted no part of it, and shut the door in his face. He was so desperate he got back to his dad's house and tried to talk me out of the bathroom. After a while I came out and I drank some green olive juice it made me so sick. I was sick a lot after that. But I'm still alive and kicking. Allen my angel, my life saver. I don't know what I would have ever done without him. We went home and didn't talk about it again. After a couple of months, we decided to have a baby. We had been married for 1 year. I went to several doctors, and they all said the same thing. Too much scar tissue you won't be able to conceive. We decided to move to North Carolina, his mom lived there, and there were specialist I could go see. By the time we got there I was already pregnant. I didn't know it yet, but I was! The doctor told me on my first Doctor visit. The excitement was so great for the both of us. We were going to have a little person to love. Pregnancy was hard, mentally, and physically. I had

dreams with all my kids during pregnancy and my body didn't want to carry them. But, by the grace of god we have 4 and their all beautiful. I called my mom to let her know she was going to be a grandma. I figured that would make everything ok between us. Maybe she had forgiven me for being so mean to her boyfriend. I had a boy; he was so tiny I loved this child from the second I knew he even existed. He was really here. I promised him that I would give him the best life and so much love. I promised him I would always believe him and I would never hurt him. I would be the best mom in the world. I couldn't get enough of that child. I wanted him with me every second of everyday. When he was 6 ½ months old we decided it was time to go home. I called my mom and asked her if she could give us $100.00 to help us get home. She sent it to us. She was dying to see my new baby. We sold what we could and packed up a back seat and the trunk full. We were on our way! We made it to Texas! We stayed at my grandma's house. Oh boy did she love that little guy. My grandma would let me and Allen sleep and she would get him out of his bed, feed him, and talk to him that little boy made my grandma so happy! Her life now revolved around that baby. We went over to my moms that next day! My mom thought he was so wonderful. I was proud; I had finally done something right in my mom's eyes! My mom helped us find a place of our own,

we had already been at grandmas for a month, and grandma had no complaints. Every time she would get on the phone she would talk about the baby. She loved playing with him he was always smiling. He never complained about nothing. My mom called and said she had found a little one bedroom. We went and looked at it when Allen got off work. We both really liked it! We bought some garage sale furniture which was great. But most of our stuff came from grandma and mom. We borrowed a TV from my little sister. Everything was wonderful. We had a party for James on his 1st birthday. My mom bought him a duck, squeaky toy. I couldn't believe that. But I was just glad she was there and part of my life. We didn't fight and she didn't have anything bad to say about me or my past. Later after the party, we went for a drive. We went through the cemetery. The same one I lived in. Allen was showing me some of the ones that had been there for a hundred years, some his family. After looking at grave stones, we pulled out. The cops pulled us over and Allen went to jail for unpaid tickets. The cops took James and I to my mom's house. My mom let me wait there for Allen to call me, and let me know when he would be home. Dale said he would be out in the morning. He said I've been to jail 3-4 times for DWI's. I'm always out the next day. He was right; Allen was out he next day. My mom came by 2 days later. She said she and

Dale had been talking and they decided that if I was going to be married to a man going to jail. They would rather not have dealings with us. I about died!

The Visit

She's with a drunk who has been to jail more than once for driving drunk and my husband had an unpaid ticket, and we are scum. I said, but it wasn't like he was driving drunk, he wasn't putting anyone in danger. She said it doesn't matter he still went to jail.

She took the TV we had borrowed from my sister. I told her Amanda said we could use it. She said yea but I paid for it. That was the end of that! Two years went by. She got sick and came knocking on my door and said I have to have surgery and I need someone to take care of the kids. Mom was running a daycare. She said they start getting there around 5:00 am. I told her I would and my dumb ass did it. I wanted to tell her NO! Remember my husband went to jail! James was now 3 and you haven't called or come by one time to see him or us. And you took away the only TV we had. But I didn't! I

agreed, told her I'd be there on Monday morning. My husband wasn't real happy but he didn't gripe at me. He just let me know he thought I should have told her to go to hell. I was at mom's at 4:45 am that Monday morning. I fed her kids, got them ready for school, took them to school, got back to get the others taken care of, mother too. She had a C-section hysterectomy. I did this all week! I would get home at around 7:00 at night. Sometimes I ask myself, why did you help her? My only answer is because it was the right thing to do. I'm not a bad person. I still tell myself that a lot even still today! After that week was finished I still kept my distance. I had a beautiful family and I realized I really didn't need her. My life was complete. I went out to see my grandma; I talked to her almost every day, and would go see her as often as I could. Grandma had started talking about grandpa one day, and she wanted to give me some of her pictures! She said I could have any I wanted. Her stories I heard a hundred times, but I still loved to hear them. Grandma started to cry and so did I because I was the one who had caused her this loneliness and I was the one who took away grandpa. I just jumped out and said it! "Grandma I am so sorry that I killed grandpa. I swear if I would have known being mean and telling him NO, I would have never said it! And I would have ate the poached eggs he made for me the next morning!" I really wanted to,

but I was being stubborn." The look on grandma's face was odd. She looked confused. She said "What are you talking about?" "My God why would you ever think you killed granddaddy?" I said because I did. She said Karm your granddaddy died because his liver was all messed up because of the liquor he use to drink. You had nothing to do with his death! Who told you, you killed him? I said Mom did! She said all of these years you thought you killed him? I said YES, I've thought about it everyday and the guilt has about killed me. Almost everytime you wanted me to come out I didn't want to because I was so ashamed of myself. And the way I hurt you and so many others. I can't begin to tell you how releaved I felt. I didn't feel ashamed anymore only relieved. I WASN'T A KILLER!!!! That day I learned a lot of things like how my mom ran off and got married, twice. How she would lie every chance she got! How she used to come in and look like she had been rode hard and hung up to dry! Lots of things! She also had told me a real hard fact. She said your mom didn't like you from the time you were born. How she wouldn't even name me, how when I had to stay in the hospital for weeks after I was born. She didn't even come up at feeding times and feed me. My grandma did. What crazy things to find out all in one day. But that also explained a lot of things to me. She also told me she knew about the beatings! She said

my mom had told her if she ever tried to come between Rick and the way I was disciplined she would never see me again! Grandma knew she meant it. So she just kept her mouth shut and tried to see me as much as she could. Grandma said she always felt bad for that! I told grandma don't feel bad any longer! Because you did what you thought was best. If you hadn't kept quiet then I wouldn't have ever had any happy things in my childhood! She said, yes but you also wouldn't have thought you killed your grandpa. I said that is ok, because I know I didn't grandma! Thank you for telling me the truth! I don't blame you for not stepping in. I thank her! My mother got married again for the sixth time. To a guy my husband always thought was gay! I liked him! By this time I had 4 kids all of them beautiful! My husband was still just as wonderful and my life was good and meaningful. My mom would call and say can we come get James and take him fishing? I would say yes he would love that! I would tell him and he would be thrilled! But my mom would never once show up to get him. That poor child would sit and wait and just cry! He didn't understand why my mother would ask and then never show up. After a lot of times of that I told him, because grandma wasn't a very nice person. She doesn't want you to go anywhere with her. I said she did the same thing to me. But you have done nothing wrong! Besides mea and dad would really miss

121

you while you were gone. When she would call and ask, I'd say sure! Knowing she would never show up, so I never told James she had called. She might have lied to me and hurt me my entire life but I was going to make sure it didn't happen to my kids. I sometimes wonder if I did the right thing, but I've always thought honesty is the best way always. This is 2006 and my mom still has never bought my kids a birthday gift! Only for James on his first birthday, the rubber duck. My little sister on the other hand her kids get whatever they want. She keeps them every weekend. That is why her 6th marriage broke up! He said it was the time in their life where they should be going and doing things. They had only been married 6 months. I don't blame him! They were in their late 40's, had money, time and could go enjoy each other. My mom said her grandbabies were more important than traveling. Finally, she picked a kid over a man! 20 years earlier would have been nice! Before she had split with her 6th husband. She came out to our house and said she was going to sell her house if unless it could stay in the family. My sister had been living with her husband a year before they were married. She said if we wanted to buy the house she would charge the same rent we were paying now! Except this would be a house we were buying. We decided to go ahead and do it! Wow our first house and we were going to own it, $250.00 per month. After 2 ½ years my door had

a knock on it. A man wanted to talk to the owner of the house. I said yes sir that's me! He asked if I was my mom? I said no! She sold it to us 2 ½ years ago. He said No you don't own this house. There is a $60,000.00 loan on this house. It belongs to them until the money is paid. I fell to my knees, weak and I told him there must be some kind of mistake. He said the tax authority had sent them papers showing that for the last year I had paid the taxes and there was ownership papers recorded at the courthouse. I said yes I told you I owned this house! He said the party that took out the loan was behind on payments and the house was being reposed, if a payment wasn't made. He went around my house taking pictures but I wouldn't let him inside. I was scared! I had never been behind on the house payments! We were paid the payments to my mom. I didn't understand any of this. I talked to my husband, and then my mom and my mom was furious. She said she didn't care where we went with my 4 kids; she wanted us out of the house immediately. We had just paid $1,100 dollars on the taxes for that year. That was twice we had paid for the taxes. I told my mother no we can't just get up and move. We bought this house from you. Mother I had to come over here by myself with my kids and clean it. Remember mom it took 2 weeks to get electric on. My kids were here in the hot summer time while I cleaned maggots out of the refrigerator.

I had to sort and pack up all of Amanda's things. Mother we worked hard to get in here. I busted my butt and you just want me to move? She said she didn't care about any of that. She said she wasn't going to jail so I'd have a place to live. Mom was right we called and found out that my mom had committed fraud. She sold us a house, took a loan out on it a couple of days before, knowing the paper work wouldn't be at the courthouse yet and then sold us the house. The police said all I had to do was bring in the ownership papers and they would take care of it from there. I wouldn't have to have any dealings with her from then on out. My husband said hell yea let's do it. I said No! He said she sold us a house that didn't even belong to her. She said you and the kids could live in the streets for all she cared. And you still won't turn her in? I said No I can't that's my mom and I don't think I can live with the guilt. I can't I'm sorry I just can't. My mom came over picked me up and we went and had some papers drawn up again. Stating that I was giving her the house back and no money exchanged just signed it over to her. Now we had to hurry to buy a house, because I believe my mom would have thrown us out on the streets. She put in her notice at the apartment she was living in. So she broke the news we had 30 days to get out. Because she was moving in. We were at her mercy because I had no legal ground to stand on. We were out in

27days. We did find another house and 6 months later we purchased it. I don't have any regrets about not turning her in. My husband could kick me in the butt, but I still have no regrets. I told my grandma what she had done and grandma said "now have you had enough?" I said yea I think so grandma! A couple of months after we had moved out my grandma told me she was going to move in with my mother. I asked her not to. She said she just couldn't make all her bills on her Social Security. So it was what she had to do. I told her to come live with us, but she said no I'm not going to intrude on you and your family. She said your mom has plenty of room, so I that is what I have chosen to do. I told her I would pay what bills she couldn't pay and she still said no. Your kids need your money, you have your own bills and family to take care of. She finally moved in with my mom. I guess things went well for her. I didn't talk to my grandma after that. Because I felt like she had stabbed me in the back. I tried not to, but I couldn't shake it. I'm not sure if I really wanted too. I had a horrible experience well my entire family did. On December 15, my house burnt from a faulty extension cord. And my little dog died a week later. And around the same time I received a phone call my grandma had a massive stroke in the road while trying to get into the car. The neighbor across the street from my mom called me to let me know. They say bad comes in

three's and I believe it does. I went to the hospital and saw my grandma. 2 hours after I left my grandma died. I visited her by her bedside for hours. I told her I was sorry for not talking to her, and I told her why. I also told her those stories about her and grandpa that I was told so many times by her. I said grandma go to grandpa he's waiting on you and he wants to dance. He wants to hold your hand again. Grandma go make more memories with grandpa and I'll see you in heaven later. And you can tell me your new stories as many times as you want. I love you and grandma thanks for being so good to me. I went home and she died after I left. You know how people say people hang on until someone tells them it is ok to go. Well I believe she was waiting on me to tell her to go to heaven. She is in heaven now I'm so lucky not only do I have God watching over me everyday, but now I have two angels watching over me too. I say that because I have been able to avoid several mishaps. For one I was going out to my father in laws one night and there were deer in the road. I slammed on my brakes, scared out of my mind, and the deer just stood there, for several minutes. After they had moved on I started driving slowly and right up the road from the deer was a huge black bull in the road. I believe if those deer hadn't been there I would have hit the bull going full speed. I got to my father in laws house and was telling him what had happened. She was upset for me and

said I'm glad you slowed down; you could have hit the bull and done some major damage to your car or killed you! There was someone who was killed on that road that night. He was driving a pick up and he hit the bull so hard that it flew up and went through the windshield. It killed the driver. See I believe grandma and grandpa put those deer in the road in front of my car, so I would have to stop. I wouldn't be here writing this. When I went in to give birth to my youngest so there were no signs of anything being wrong. The Doctor come in and said he would be back in a little bit, he needed a shower. He had been at the gym working out! In just a few minutes he was back still dressed in the same clothes. He told the nurse that he wanted me prepared for surgery within 10 minutes. He asked me if I believed in God. I said yes! He said do you believe in Angels. I said "Yes sir I do!" He said on my way home I had an angel whisper in my ear telling me to go back. You must go now or she will die, go back! He came right back alright. I just got chills! He talked to my family waiting outside and before I knew it I was being wheeled into surgery. Doc said that if we had waited another 5 minutes. The baby would have drown in my blood and I would hemorrhaged to death. God my grandpa were there, God has a purpose for me! I think writing this book is my purpose to tell my story and help others who had to live in hell as a child. Because of the

127

mental, physical, or sexual abuse, I want people to know that there is a God and he loves each and every one of us. He is always there! You are never alone! My favorite poem is "Foot Prints in the Sand"! I believe God carried me my whole life I wasn't ever alone, and he didn't give me more than I could handle. I'm writing this book and I know in my heart that it will help others. God gave me friends who had the means to get me out of bad situations. My husband is a gift from God! He is a beautiful man who has put up with me, and my screwed up head. He has put up with my mood swings, yelling, throwing things, and me being afraid of everything! He has also put up with my choices. Honey, I love you! My tantrums, and all the rest of my faults over the last 18 years. And my children, they are the biggest blessing of all. I love them unconditionally just as they do me. I have beautiful friends, they are there for me, and they know without question that I will be there whenever they need me. God has blessed me my whole life it just took me a long time to see that. I have done a lot of soul searching. Yes, I found out I have a soul, I am not a child of the devil, I am a child of God. He has taught me to forgive, to be good to others even when there are not so good to me. He has taught me that I have no grounds to judge. He is our only judge. I have forgiven all those who have hurt me. I have discovered new standards I don't believe in failure. And

I don't believe that there should be excuses for everytime somebody messes up. I don't believe in weakeness, I feel if you ask God will give you all the strength you need. I am proof! I have made a wonderful life for myself and all in my life. I feel when people feel sorry for you it makes you weak. I don't think people should feel sorry for themselves. I think they should hold up there heads and say I am a good person! Stop using their past as an excuse for their wrong doing. Drugs, beating, their own children, abusing them mentally and physically, they need to stop the pattern. Do right by their children and the ones that are in their life. It can be done! I am proof like so many others. Don't ask why me? There is a purpose, even though it is hard to see. Get up and do something with your life. For your family, your friends, and most of all for yourself! Reach inside you and say I am no longer going to follow the footsteps of my parents or whoever it was that hurt you! Take a stand. Take a different road, stop feeling sorry for yourself. Don't abuse yourself by the guilt of your past. Forgive yourself and you will find peace. Ask God to help you and I promise you he will! He is waiting on you to make the first move. And he has never left your side. Make a change, No more excuses, just do it! It stops today! You are the one to make this step! One day at a time, and it can be done! Remember that things aren't your fault! You know there

is strength in other people's weakness! I found strength through the weakness of my mom, dad, and Rick. Somehow their weakness made me even stronger. I cry now, I hug now, I let people know they are good. I tell them they have done a good job, I try to encourage people! I find it very rewarding! I have learned how to love everyone! And even though I sometimes feel God short changed me on "brains", book wise he gave me the brains I needed for life. I feel I am a good person to be around. I feel that I do make a difference. I learned from my parents and step dad a lot. I learned how not to be. I learned to be me! A good person, with heart and soul! I AM A SURVIVOR!

www.ingramcontent.com/pod-product-compliance
Lightning Source LLC
Chambersburg PA
CBHW020242290526
45784CB00003B/1078